Continental Philosophy and Theology

Theology

Editor-in-Chief

Stephan van Erp (*KU Leuven, Belgium*)

Associate Editors

Christian Bauer (*University of Innsbruck*)
Judith Gruber (*KU Leuven, Belgium*)
David Grumett (*University of Edinburgh*)
Paul Hedges (*Nanyang Technological University, Singapore*)
Vincent Lloyd (*Villanova University*)

Volumes published in this Brill Research Perspectives title are listed at *brill.com/rpth*

Continental Philosophy and Theology

By

Colby Dickinson

BRILL

LEIDEN | BOSTON

This paperback book edition is simultaneously published as issue 2.1 (2018) of *Theology*, DOI 10.1163/24683493-12340003.

The Library of Congress Cataloging-in-Publication Data is available online at http://catalog.loc.gov
LC record available at http://lccn.loc.gov/2018940582

Typeface for the Latin, Greek, and Cyrillic scripts: "Brill". See and download: brill.com/brill-typeface.

ISBN 978-90-04-36127-0 (paperback)
ISBN 978-90-04-37603-8 (e-book)

Copyright 2018 by Colby Dickinson. Published by Koninklijke Brill NV, Leiden, The Netherlands.
Koninklijke Brill NV incorporates the imprints Brill, Brill Hes & De Graaf, Brill Nijhoff, Brill Rodopi, Brill Sense and Hotei Publishing.
Koninklijke Brill NV reserves the right to protect the publication against unauthorized use and to authorize dissemination by means of offprints, legitimate photocopies, microform editions, reprints, translations, and secondary information sources, such as abstracting and indexing services including databases. Requests for commercial re-use, use of parts of the publication, and/or translations must be addressed to Koninklijke Brill NV.

This book is printed on acid-free paper and produced in a sustainable manner.

Printed by Printforce, the Netherlands

Contents

Continental Philosophy and Theology 1
 Colby Dickinson
 Abstract 1
 Keywords 1
 Introduction 1
 Part 1: The Political-Theological Stakes of Continental Thought 12
  Sovereignty and the Subversion of Christendom 12
  Martin Heidegger and the Attempt to Overcome Metaphysics 21
 Part 2: Reassessing the Dualisms within Political Theology 29
  The Well-Founded Fears of Apostasy and Transgression within Continental Philosophy 29
  The 'Endless' Deconstruction of Identity 33
  The Perpetual Political Theological Complaint against the Negativity of Continental Philosophy 38
  Communitarian Opposition to the Genealogists 41
  The Other Side of Things 45
 Part 3: Continental Thought beyond Dualistic Thinking 50
  Representative Dichotomies or Antinomies of Thought 51
  Rethinking the Role of Negativity in Continental Philosophy 58
  William Desmond and Diana Eck on Porousness 65
  Joeri Schrijvers on a Ground between Faith and Belief 70
  A Phenomenological Way Forward 74
 Conclusion 79
 Bibliography 82
  Primary Texts 82
  Secondary Texts 93
  Book Series 103

Continental Philosophy and Theology

Colby Dickinson
Loyola University Chicago, USA
cdickinson1@luc.edu

Abstract

Continental philosophy underwent a 'return to religion' or a 'theological turn' in the late 20th Century. And yet any conversation between continental philosophy and theology must begin by addressing the perceived distance between them: that one is concerned with destroying all normative, metaphysical order (continental philosophy's task) and the other with preserving religious identity and community in the face of an increasingly secular society (theology's task). Colby Dickinson argues in *Continental Philosophy and Theology* rather that perhaps such a tension is constitutive of the nature of order, thinking and representation which typically take dualistic forms and which might be rethought, though not necessarily abolished. Such a shift in perspective even allows one to contemplate this distance as not opting for one side over the other or by striking a middle ground, but as calling for a nondualistic theology that measures the complexity and inherently comparative nature of theological inquiry in order to realign theology's relationship to continental philosophy entirely.

Keywords

continental philosophy – political theology – Martin Heidegger – Carl Schmitt – Søren Kierkegaard – metaphysics – phenomenology – dualism – sovereignty – messianic

Introduction

Broadly construed, continental philosophy underwent something of a shift in emphasis in the late 20th Century that various commentators working within the field have, with some distinction, described as a 'return to religion' or a 'theological turn'. As has become apparent, the epistemological focus undertaken within modernity (Descartes, Kant, Hegel) eventually yielded to a genealogical investigation of the 'origins' of morality and conceptual thought (Nietzsche) as well as a phenomenological turn toward the 'things themselves' (Husserl, Heidegger) which itself evolved into an ontological-existential reconfiguration of Being (Kierkegaard, Heidegger, Sartre, Merleau-Ponty). Subsequently as these philosophies declared new methods and insights, continental thought was also modified by a 'linguistic turn' (the 'later Heidegger', Wittgenstein, Derrida, Foucault) and, roughly contemporaneous, an 'ethical turn' (Levinas) as well. In one instance, Jean-François Lyotard's ability to combine linguistic structural problematics alongside ethical imperatives in his *Le Différend*—one of the major French philosophical works of the past century—is an excellent testimony to how such turns are in reality not entirely separate movements, but rather envelope one another and altogether overlap in their attempt to explore the complex nature of how existence evolves in multiple dimensions at once.[1] Much of the works of Gilles Deleuze, Jacques Derrida and Michel Foucault, for example, evidence similarly intertwined combinations of thought. Though each of these turns eventually yielded to a religious or theological turn, isolating and identifying the individual strains of each 'turn' can be helpful, no matter how incomplete a singular perspective might be in the face of multiple but essentially similar trends. From this perspective, taking a moment to discuss the 'turn' to religion or theological subjects within continental philosophy can be instrumental in seeing where continental philosophy and theology converge in potentially unexpected ways in a contemporary context. Such a context of a 'theological turn' within continental philosophy is, in many ways, what I take to be main focus of the present work.

Though a host of writers working in the United States had already been progressing toward such a theological turn—John Caputo, Richard Kearney and Merold Westphal spring readily to mind—philosophers working in French, German and Italian contexts had themselves instigated a profound shift in emphasis that would signal a deliberate reckoning with the impact that the Jewish and Christian legacies in the West specifically had made upon our comprehension of the (western) structures of thought and being. In many ways, the early to mid-20th Century fragmentation of continental philosophy into a variety of seemingly separate fields such as phenomenology, critical theory, existentialism, genealogy-archaeology, hermeneutics, particular psychoanalytic and Marxist schools of thought and deconstructionism was essentially given the chance to interconnect these loose and often apparently disparate strands of inquiry through a common probe into religiously inflected themes. At the

---

1 Jean-François Lyotard, *The Differend: Phrases in Dispute*, trans. Georges Van Den Abbeele (Minneapolis, MN: University of Minnesota Press, 1988).

same time, however, such a shared focus is difficult to sustain, as we will see, since most of these philosophical trends are decidedly critical, or negative, in their approach, whereas the theological always seems to maintain something of a positive, constructive (or even *revealed*) outlook. Those working in the various fields and subfields of theology are for this reason still trying to assess the impact which such philosophical study has made upon its own reflections and propositions. The present work is but one instance of such an ongoing assessment.

The theological turn within continental philosophy was perhaps inaugurated by Martin Heidegger's influential attempts to overcome the lasting impact of onto-theology in the West—that is, to reconceive entirely the ill-conjoined Greek-Christian metaphysical legacy in order to critique the notions of logic or order that undergird the language-*logos* configuration that humanity has been so dependent on for its collective existence (and which the history of theology seems to confirm, as the subsequent investigations of Giorgio Agamben and Roberto Esposito, among others, have recently noted).[2] What Heidegger was trying to isolate specifically was what we often take for granted: that order itself, as the rationality of a given community and so the foundation for ethical and political interactions, is instituted through its ability to exclude or marginalize certain elements, and that such activities were predicated on, and legitimated by, certain metaphysical-theological propositions. In his analysis, the 'as' structure—taking something 'as' something in particular—is the foundation of our understanding, and is as such based on a logic of representations (*logos*) that thrusts humanity into an either/or dichotomy of types (the basis of all categorizations).[3] Many of the dualisms that structure western philosophical and theological thought (e.g. necessity/contingency, sovereignty/democracy, grace/law, among others) are caught up in particular representational logics that structure our world and the actions of humans within it. Critiquing metaphysics, therefore, *by definition*, meant also critiquing the existence and function of such dualisms and the ways in which they structured the various

---

2 See, in particular, Martin Heidegger, *An Introduction to Metaphysics*, trans. Ralph Manheim (New Haven, CT: Yale University Press, 1959). See also Giorgio Agamben, *The Kingdom and the Glory: For a Theological Genealogy of Economy and Government*, trans. Lorenzo Chiesa with Matteo Mandarini (Stanford: Stanford University Press, 2011) and Roberto Esposito, *Two: The Machine of Political Theology and the Place of Thought*, trans. Zakiya Hanafi (New York: Fordham University Press, 2015).

3 Martin Heidegger, *Logic: The Question of Truth*, trans. Thomas Sheehan (Bloomington, IN: Indiana University Press, 2010), pp. 126–128, 116–117. The dichotomies that Heidegger culls from Aristotle's categories includes *synthesis/diairesis* (synthesizing/separating), *alethes/pseudos* (uncovering/covering-over), and *kataphasis/apophasis* (affirming/denying).

coordinates of power within a given field (e.g. politics, economics, religion, society, philosophy and so on).

Heidegger's bid for the destruction of metaphysics began a longstanding initiative in continental thought to eradicate the influence of metaphysics— what Jacques Derrida, following Heidegger very closely in this regard, referred to as a 'phallo-logo-centrism' at the heart of onto-theology. Derrida too had sought throughout his lifetime to isolate, de-construct and point beyond such configurations, though not to a particular, concrete or historical form, but only to an empty horizon of justice always yet 'to come'.[4] The Heideggerian assault on onto-theology was so influential that multiple philosophers (and theologians) immediately came under its spell and sought in their works to jettison any previously unconscious dependency on metaphysical propositions that likewise indebted one to certain politically sovereign, and often exclusive or violent, representational forms (e.g. such as a sovereign, omnipotent God who acts out of necessity and predestines every occurrence, but which really conceals human exploits for power, wealth and to defend the status quo).

As has been highly persuasive in academia throughout recent decades, a critique analogous to Heidegger's was put forth by Michel Foucault, among others, whose questioning of established paradigms of order (including the order imposed within Christianity through pastoral power) was fundamental to his archaeology of western religious thought and its ability to create 'abnormal' and 'deviant' types through the hegemonic order it helped cement as the typical western rationality.[5] Christianity, in his eyes, had played a central role in constructing a dominant and moral narrative that gave order to the world, certainly, but which also confined the human being to a rather limited identity (e.g. in terms of sexuality, gender, race, citizenship and so on) rather than explore the possibilities of living in a state of freedom beyond such imposed logics. In this sense, both Foucault and Heidegger were attempting, like their mentor Friedrich Nietzsche before them, to overcome those metaphysical-theological constructions that had bequeathed a certain rationality to the West through established religious logics.[6] In many ways, this Nietzschean trajectory

---

4 See Jacques Derrida, *Dissemination*, trans. Barbara Johnson (Chicago: University of Chicago Press, 1981). See also his lectures on, *Heidegger: The Question of Being and History*, ed. Thomas Dutoit, trans. Geoffrey Bennington (Chicago: University of Chicago Press, 2016).
5 Michel Foucault, *The Order of Things: An Archaeology of the Human Sciences* (New York: Vintage, 1994). See also Robert Nichols, *The World of Freedom: Heidegger, Foucault, and the Politics of Historical Ontology* (Stanford: Stanford University Press, 2014).
6 Foucault, in one of his lectures, even cites approvingly the work of Paul Feyerabend, whose book *Against Method* eschews systematic-scientific rigor in the hopes of accessing a space

brought about a sustained revaluation of all values in the West through what appeared at first as their destruction (or de-construction, in Derrida's favored parlance).

As is commonly discussed amongst those more critical of 20th Century or postmodern continental philosophy, these efforts to overcome metaphysics and the almost sacred bonds of normative order they have inspired have often left readers wondering if there were anything redeemable to be found in philosophical thought other than a permanent and negative critique of whatever subject was under analysis. Continental philosophy, for this reason, has often appeared to some as being either a wholly nihilistic exercise with no concrete goals of its own, an orgiastic reveling in an ephemeral, antinomian celebration of the end of all governing norms (Nietzsche's Dionysian exuberance, Foucault's sadomasochistic hopes) *or* as a pointing toward a horizon of 'better things' that will never actually appear as a reality in our world (Derrida's messianic deconstructionism). For some, then, like Theodor Adorno, philosophy was the space needing to be left permanently open so that the critical powers of thought might always be able to function.[7] For others, like Georges Bataille, the push for an excessive transgression of any normative order almost gave birth to a new sense of sacrality—one that held forth dramatic possibilities for liberation, though it seemed also never to deliver on its promises in the 'real world'.[8]

The more recent work of the French theorist René Girard on violence and the sacred has given rise to what is essentially a parallel suggestion to this line of inquiry, though beginning with vastly differing methods, source texts and presumptions: communities formulate their sense of order or 'peace' through the exclusion of a scapegoat or innocent victim who is deemed to have transgressed a particular social-sacred norm or boundary. Moving beyond the mimetic (imitative) contagion that would posit a collective, unanimous violence as (for some) *the* source of sacrality in our world—such is Girard's thesis— means that we cannot locate the means of overcoming such violence in *this* world, hence the apparently transcendent quality of finding the means to

---

beyond the merely 'rational'. Michel Foucault, *On the Government of the Living: Lectures at the Collège de France, 1979–1980*, ed. Michel Senellart, trans. Graham Burchell (Basingstoke: Palgrave Macmillan, 2014), p. 79. See also Paul Feyerabend, *Against Method* (London: Verso, 1975).

7 See how this stance unfolds in his essays gathered in Theodor W. Adorno, *Critical Models: Interventions and Catchwords*, trans. Henry W. Pickford (New York: Columbia University Press, 1998).

8 Georges Bataille, *Theory of Religion*, trans. Robert Hurley (New York: Zone, 1992).

overcome violence, order and whatever normative representation we are presented with.[9] At the same time, that which overcomes such violence appears to us as a 'most radical weakness'.[10] Hence, as a prominent Girardian and theologian James Alison has noted, our conceptualizations of order and reason, not to mention our cultural and political institutions, are grounded in (more or less) violent exclusions—a point that Foucault strove hard to make in a number of his writings.[11] This claim is made, however, not to suggest that we are able to live *without* order—what Girard relates to the notion of 'belonging'— as if suspended in a permanently antinomian reality (and what many critics of continental thought have generally take to be the main result of anyone following this seemingly nihilistic Nietzschean legacy). Belonging, in Girard's eyes, should be neither a univocal or unilateral decision, which is the mistake of both 'right-wing and left-wing ideologies', nor something to be 'thrown off at all costs', as some revolutionary theories suggest.[12] What Girard hints at is that belonging is a complex phenomenon that involves something like a 'relational ontology', as Andrew Benjamin has described it, that takes a greater and an ever more accurate account of the complexities and frustrations of identity and life.[13] Such a balanced perspective typically lingers underneath even the most boisterous philosophical critiques of normative order, though not every

---

9   René Girard, *I See Satan Fall Like Lightning*, trans. James G. Williams (Maryknoll, NY: Orbis, 2001), p. 189. See too the commentary offered in Scott Cowdell, *René Girard and Secular Modernity: Christ, Culture, and Crisis* (Notre Dame, IN: University of Notre Dame Press, 2013).

10 Girard, *I See Satan Fall Like Lightning*, p. 143.

11 James Alison, *Faith Beyond Resentment: Fragments Catholic and Gay* (New York: Crossroad, 2001), pp. 134, 154. See also René Girard, *Things Hidden Since the Fondation of the World*, pp. 48–83. For an instructive reading of Girardian thought in relation to ecclesiology, see Grant Kaplan, *René Girard, Unlikely Apologist: Mimetic Theory and Fundamental Theology* (Notre Dame, IN: University of Notre Dame Press, 2016).

12 René Girard, 'Belonging', trans. Rob Grayson, *Contagion* 23 (2016), pp. 1–12, p. 11.

13 As it pertains to the dichotomies and genealogical/phenomenological methodologies, it is perhaps helpful to note Benjamin's definition of a relational ontology as well: 'Relationality, now understood in terms of an original relationality, has always been a possibility within the history of philosophy. Nonetheless, it is often excised to position modes of singularity as primary. However, that excision can be undone such that the recovery and possible affirmation of relationality becomes philosophy's other possibility. Uncovering that original relationality presupposed its presence as a potentiality, and therefore integral to its recovery was the development of what are called counter-measures'. Andrew Benjamin, *Towards a Relational Ontology: Philosophy's Other Possibility* (Albany, NY: State University of New York Press, 2015), p. 217.

critic of continental thought, or *even the continental philosophers themselves*, are frequently wont to admit as much.¹⁴

Seeing how Heidegger and Girard somewhat converge in their challenges to the concepts of order and logic within our world might help us to make sense of why someone as radical in their political and atheistic thought as Slavoj Žižek has recently been able to maintain something like a direct fidelity to both authors in his work.¹⁵ It might also help us to understand why so many philosophers—with a good number of presumed and stated atheists among them—might have taken such an interest in more overtly theological topics within the last 30 years or so, as the destruction of one idea of the sacred almost inevitably gives rise to possibilities for another form to reemerge.

Though the insights of Heidegger, Foucault, Derrida and even Girard were generally not considered enough to merit them being a 'religious turn' in and of themselves in the 20th Century, such insights have opened a path directly toward the religious upon which many other continental thinkers have subsequently traveled. A variety of phenomenological writers in the late 20th Century, for example, have found a number of ways to produce conversation on theological elements within human experience that have found significant overlap with pre-existing theological themes. The writings of Emmanuel Levinas, Jean-Luc Marion, Jean-Yves Lacoste, Jean-Louis Chrétien, Michel Henry and more have all pointed toward phenomenological methods and conclusions that resonate deeply with specifically theological themes and, in turn, offer theological discourse the opportunity to reflect critically upon its own operations and positions.¹⁶ As I will take up at the end of the present study, such pathways have offered us some of the most significant philosophical-theological considerations in recent memory. In some ways this is the case because they often do not seek to overcome one side in a dualistic schema in order to endorse another, but because they seek somehow to preserve both sides—a point that frequently gets them labeled as too conservative or religious in their work, but which may end up being too an often mistaken impression.

---

14   I explore these themes more directly in my *Between the Canon and the Messiah: The Structure of Faith in Contemporary Continental Thought* (London: Bloomsbury, 2013).
15   See Slavoj Žižek, *The Ticklish Subject: The Absent Centre of Political Ontology* (London: Verso, 1999) as well as Slavoj Žižek, *Less Than Nothing: Hegel and the Shadow of Dialectical Materialism* (London: Verso, 2012).
16   See, among others, Dominique Janicaud, et al., *Phenomenology and the Theological Turn: The French Debate* (New York: Fordham University Press, 2001) as well as Hent de Vries, *Philosophy and the Turn to Religion* (Baltimore, MD: John Hopkins University Press, 1999).

At almost the same time as such strains of phenomenology were pursuing theological topics, the various returns to the letters of Saint Paul became evidence as well that other strands of continental thought could likewise begin to re-examine post-Heideggerian attempts to overcome traditional metaphysics vis-à-vis historical religious efforts to restructure our relationship to Being. In many ways, these readings of Saint Paul became a way to extend the excessive transgressions of earlier writers, such as Heidegger and Foucault, into the domain of the religious, thereby putting them at odds with the phenomenologists in some sense. The short works of Jacob Taubes, Stanislas Breton, Alain Badiou, Giorgio Agamben and Slavoj Žižek all explored how Pauline thought, or Saint Paul's reconfiguration of Jesus' teaching, might be read as transgressive of normative identities and how this early founder of Christianity may have actually been exploring important philosophical themes in his otherwise ostensibly religious works.[17] Such readings of Pauline thought have opened our eyes toward the antinomian flavor of continental philosophy in general (in Taubes and Agamben's readings in particular) as well as the creation of a militant subjectivity (in Badiou and Žižek).

Following fast on the heels of such examinations, the publication and translations of Heidegger's lectures on Paul, Jean-Luc Nancy's radical deconstruction of Christianity, Ted Jenning's efforts to reread Derrida in light of Pauline thought, Simon Critchley's attempt to establish the 'faith of the faithless', not to mention all the commentaries and critiques of this quickly evolving discourse, soon quickly sped this philosophical-Pauline trajectory toward a much more theologically-inclined audience that was eager to further deconstruct theological and dogmatic norms.[18] In many ways, philosophers and theologians alike

---

17 Giorgio Agamben, *The Time that Remains: A Commentary on the Letter to the Romans*, trans. Patricia Dailey (Stanford: Stanford University Press, 2005), Alain Badiou, *Saint Paul: The Foundation of Universalism*, trans. Ray Brassier (Stanford: Stanford University Press, 2003), Stanislas Breton, *A Radical Philosophy of Saint Paul*, trans. Joseph N. Ballan (New York: Columbia University Press, 2011), Jacob Taubes, *The Political Theology of Paul*, trans. Dana Hollander (Stanford: Stanford University Press, 2004) as well as Žižek, *The Ticklish Subject*.

18 See Martin Heidegger, *The Phenomenology of Religious Life*, trans. Matthias Fritsch and Jennifer Anna Gosetti-Ferencei (Bloomington, IN: Indiana University Press, 2004), Jean-Luc Nancy, *Dis-Enclosure: The Deconstruction of Christianity*, trans. Bettina Bergo, Gabriel Malenfant, and Michael B. Smith (New York: Fordham University Press, 2008), Theodore W. Jennings, Jr., *Reading Derrida / Thinking Paul: On Justice* (Stanford: Stanford University Press, 2005) and Simon Critchley, *Faith of the Faithless: Experiments in Political Theology* (London: Verso, 2012). See also John D. Caputo and Linda Martín Alcoff, eds., *Paul Among the Philosophers* (Bloomington, IN: Indiana University Press, 2009) and

are still contemplating the consequences of such readings and what implications they hold, if any, for theological and religious doctrines, practices and identities.

Some of the most noticeable traits of these theologically-significant and philosophically deconstructive writings, especially among the Pauline commentators, are the political elements that have been brought to the forefront of the general conversation. That is, the context wherein the 'theological turn' has occurred has swiftly been noted as simultaneously bearing a re-examination of the domain of the political at the same moment as the religious, giving rise to a unique focus on political-theological themes within continental philosophical discussions. Hence, it has become impossible to study the works of Walter Benjamin, Giorgio Agamben, Jean-Luc Nancy, Alain Badiou, Judith Butler, Gianni Vattimo, Simon Critchley or Slavoj Žižek without reference to the field of political theology in some fashion. This reality has brought a variety of young political theologians into deeper and noteworthy contact with continental philosophy, including Jeffrey Robbins, Clayton Crockett, Ward Blanton and Noëlle Vahanian, among others.[19]

Taking each of these trends together, a number of illustrative theses have come to light as a result of such philosophical 'turns' toward the religious or the theological, which I believe could be summarized (though certainly not exhaustively) as follows: firstly, the commentary on Pauline thought essentially boils down to a discussion of the structures of thought, identity and existence that very much continues the ongoing, and at times genealogical, deconstruction of metaphysics. For example, we are able to follow these interpretations of Paul in seeing how antinomian impulses are the necessary result of any given normative identity or order (Taubes), hence all identities are subdivided from within (Agamben), and yet the self makes an all-important (political) decision to remain faithful to the Event that disrupted its previous existence in order to constitute a new form of subjectivity (Badiou). There is little effort made in such writings, however, toward contributing a positive sense of what a community or identity should look like, as this falls outside the scope of their intended criticisms.

Secondly, there is a final concession, made most prominently by Agamben in his conclusion to his *Homo Sacer* series, *The Use of Bodies*, that the time

---

Gregg Lambert, *Return Statements: The Return of Religion in Contemporary Philosophy* (Edinburgh: Edinburgh University Press, 2016).

19 For a general overview of such interactions, see Ward Blanton, Clayton Crockett, Jeffrey W. Robbins and Noëlle Vahanian, *An Insurrectionist Manifesto: Four New Gospels for a Radical Politics* (New York: Columbia University Press, 2016).

for isolated 'turns' is perhaps over, as we are now able to realize that one cannot make ontological formulations without recognizing that they are at the same time ethical, political, economic *and* religious.[20] In other words, we are not able to isolate one aspect of philosophical or theological thought at the expense of another. For this reason, theological subjects will need to be scrutinized as much as economic or political ones as we continue to investigate western models of thought. Such a conclusion resonates quite deeply, it should also be noted, with current work being done on the complexity of systems and networks, such as we find in Bruno Latour's thought.[21] For Latour, systems of networks operate beyond any hierarchical representations of order—a point that allows us to assess entire fields of study, and their presumed methodologies, anew.

Thirdly, there is an implicit recognition within numerous continental writers' works that our material reality is 'not all' there is to existence. Whether viewed from the perspective of the 'saturated phenomena' (Marion), the 'liturgical reduction' of our world (Lacoste), as the poverty of existence (Agamben) or as a rift within existence itself (Žižek), each author points toward an opening to that which goes beyond our perceived, or represented, reality. Each of these thinkers, though there are many more I might mention, implicitly follows Heidegger's reading of the ek-static nature of our existence or being-there (*Dasein*) that throws us beyond ourselves, but which also begins from within the limited confines of existence itself. It is for this reason that such work is still carried on underneath Heidegger's shadow, as problematic and contested as his legacy continues to be.[22] For others, however, such an ek-static nature of existence is also the very condition of our being that points us toward the divine—though not everyone will follow this path of speculation.

What I argue in the chapters that follow is essentially that any conversation between continental philosophy and theology must begin at the present moment by acknowledging how their mutual interaction has been impeded at times by the presumption that there is an impossible distance between the two fields, that one is concerned with destroying all normative 'sacred' (metaphysical) order and the other with preserving religious identity and community in

---

20 Giorgio Agamben, *The Use of Bodies*, trans. Adam Kotsko (Stanford: Stanford University Press, 2015).

21 Bruno Latour, *An Inquiry into Modes of Existence: An Anthropology of the Moderns*, trans. Catherine Porter (Cambridge, MA: Harvard University Press, 2013).

22 One of the more recent engagements with the implications of Heidegger's 'Black Notebooks' and legacy in general is Mårten Björk and Jayne Svenungsson, eds., *Heidegger's Black Notebooks and the Future of Theology* (London: Palgrave Macmillan, 2017).

the face of an increasingly secular society. Though not every theological voice would share in such a view, to be sure, this perceived gap has functioned as one of the greatest obstacles to their mutual dialogue in the modern period. Hence, the apparent impasse between the deconstructive genealogists who endlessly ('nihilistically') destroy whatever foundation had seemed to be most solid under our feet and the communitarians who rely upon the decisionism of sovereign power in order to establish the foundations of communal identity (and all identitarian representations) is a very real and present tension to be sure (as many have staked their careers on fighting for one side against the other), but it is also a misunderstanding of the way in which dualisms can and should be addressed in our world. That is, it is the nature of things like order, thinking and representation which typically take dualistic (and frequently metaphysical) forms that must be rethought, though not necessarily abolished. Hence, the genealogist/communitarian tension, undergirded by the sovereign/democratic dualism, as I will here describe it, must be perceived anew, not as something that can be easily overcome, but as the inherent and ineradicable way things work. Such a shift in perspective might allow us too, as it has allowed many continental philosophers recently, to contemplate different ways of dealing with dualistic thinking other than simply opting for one side over the other, or by impossibly trying to strike a middle position that never seems to hold in the end.

Part one will therefore begin to unpack this impossible tension by returning to one of its modern sources: the either/or dichotomy for faith championed by Søren Kierkegaard, developed in a political context by Carl Schmitt and philosophically elaborated by Martin Heidegger. My aim is to demonstrate how such a challenge to philosophical thought has been highly influential upon various theological strains of thought and how we might need to reconsider the dominance of such an either/or dichotomy. The second part pursues this either/or dichotomy as it has become embedded in both continental philosophical lines of thought, particularly in its genealogical or deconstructivist forms such as in the writings of Jacques Derrida, and in (theological) communitarian propositions. By tracing this dualistic lineage as it manifests itself in each camp as a sort of political theology, I hope to show how we might be able to begin thinking differently about this tension and look toward more creative ways to deal with the inescapable reality of utilizing dualistic thinking in order to have a shared sense of intelligibility at all (i.e. linguistic, religious, political, representational and so on). In the final part, then, I am able to address the various and contested uses of dualistic concepts within theological and philosophical thought in both modern and contemporary history. By isolating and critiquing the political usage of such dualisms, I point to various efforts to move toward a nondualistic way of performing theology as a type of critical political theology working in tandem with continental philosophical insights.

My aim is ultimately to develop a methodology that attempts to assess the political implementation of dualistic representations and thereby to find ways to think both philosophically and so also theologically in a nondualistic manner while also conceding the necessity of dualistic thinking for representational purposes. It is my hope that such research will enable a more sustainable engagement with (1) the historical and political uses of such dualisms alongside various parallel attempts to think 'nondualistically' and (2) the establishment of a theology that deals with the existence of complexity and comparison within theological matters in a more realistic manner. Though the apparent obviousness of the political use of dualisms remains, little work has been done to unmask the political theological dimensions of such usage and to point toward a more constructive, critical account of the theological in relation to the political. Taking steps toward formulating a nondualistic theology that more accurately measures the complexity and inherently comparative nature of theological inquiry is therefore an essential task remaining before us.

Part 1: The Political-Theological Stakes of Continental Thought

Sovereignty and the Subversion of Christendom

Contemporary theology, for its part, still lives somewhat under the shadow of what Gary Dorrien has called the 'Barthian revolt in modern theology',[23] a now somewhat diverse phenomenon that shares at least this much in common throughout its various incarnations: the sovereignty of God is well-preserved and kept at a safe distance from the world and its political affairs. Or, generally speaking, this is what is most often presumed to be the case. A counterargument could be formulated, however, that no notion of sovereignty, whether God's, the State's, the Pope's (in Catholicism) or the autonomous individual's (as is frequently the case in Protestantism), can be established apart from the realm of a very this-worldly politics. Taking up the sovereignty of God as a central tenet in one's theology is therefore inseparably wedded to a host of conceptual linkages that cannot be so easily dismissed as irrelevant to theopolitical speculation. In fact, a cornucopia of concepts could be said to descend directly from God's sovereignty, including necessity, decision, autonomy,

---

23   Gary Dorrien, *The Barthian Revolt in Modern Theology: Theology without Weapons* (Louisville, KY: Westminster John Knox Press, 1999).

authority, glory and transcendence, to name but some. Ascertaining the various interactions between such concepts and the political consequences for theological thought of their usage is what contemporary political theologians have often scrambled to demonstrate.

The Swiss theologian Karl Barth's attempt to ground all theological reflection in the Word of God understood as entirely autonomous from worldly affairs, very much appears from a certain political theological angle as *the* (sovereign) decision that establishes its foundations *ex nihilo*, what the political jurist Carl Schmitt had argued in a very different context was necessary for the sovereign to appear *as* sovereign and thereby to ground all existing forms of law.[24] For Schmitt, of course, this had meant searching to find justification for papal sovereignty and Catholic monarchical forms over the rise of liberal-democratic states, *but also* for the dictatorial power of the Nazi Führer—Schmitt's personal and scholarly downfall.[25] The fact that many today still attempt to study Barth's pronouncements apart from Schmitt's work—as if the one formulation of sovereignty had nothing to do with the other—should prompt serious concern for theologians of all confessions and commitments, but also a pressing desire to consider anew what the implications of (political) sovereignty are for the study of theological conceptualizations of the divine. Such influence, however, is not limited to forms of sovereignty alone.

One can also locate a perhaps benign parallel to Schmitt's attacks on (political) liberalism in Barth's frustration with 19th Century liberal theology, of which Friedrich Schleiermacher was the so-called 'father', as well as in his desire to reassert the sovereign voice of God's Word (or, more cynically, perhaps, the theologian's) in a variety of pronouncements. Having to abandon its true source of determining power—the real fault of liberalism—theology was, in Barth's eyes, forced into an 'apologetic corner' from which it merely hoped that others would find its appeals to faith convincing, despite its having lost, once and for all, a real, and often rationally justifiable, metaphysical strength.[26] Though Barth himself would not attempt to reinstate any premodern justifications for

---

24   Carl Schmitt, *Political Theology: Four Chapters on the Concept of Sovereignty*, trans. George Schwab (Chicago: University of Chicago Press, 1985).

25   See, among others, Carl Schmitt, *The Crisis of Parliamentary Democracy*, trans. Ellen Kennedy (Cambridge, MA: MIT Press, 1985). See the commentary offered on Schmitt, as well as Heidegger, in Yvonne Sherratt, *Hitler's Philosophers* (New Haven, CT: Yale University Press, 2013).

26   'This formulation of the problem was brought about by the embarrassing situation—the 'apologetic corner'—into which modern theology, with decreasing power of resistance, has allowed itself to be pushed, through the rise of a conceited and self-sufficient humanity, a tendency to be observed in its advance from Pietism through the Enlightenment to

a rational metaphysical system—indeed in a post-Heideggerian context it was increasingly difficult to do so—he was mainly concerned to overcome this liberal theological deficit by refocusing things on the surpassing, sovereign Word situated above all human words. Schmitt too had found some solace in arguing for the absolute position of 'strong' sovereign over against his 'weak' liberal 'enemies'.

The work of the early Barth was inspired, as is well-documented, by the writings of the Danish theologian Søren Kierkegaard. Kierkegaard had previously found himself in a very unusual religious and political situation of being published in the midst of a 19th Century European Christendom where national churches were the norm and every citizen declared a Christian by birth, though with far fewer persons actually taking their faith seriously. It was Kierkegaard's emphatic distance taken from the Church, Christendom, the State and even democracy alike, it could be contended, that opened up a door for theologians such as Barth to wager their speculations upon an absolute distinction between God and humanity that actually ended up re-doubling the stakes of the political within what appeared to be solely the domain of the metaphysical—what certain forms of political theology today tell us is really a finely interwoven and necessary relationship that often conceals or distorts its proximate connections.

Kierkegaard's appeal to later theologians, especially those working in a Barthian framework, often would be predicated upon his various 'attacks upon Christendom' wherein he sought to emphasize the individual's ability to overcome centuries of distance from the person of Christ in order to be 'contemporaneous' with him and to experience the Word of God firsthand as a challenge to complacent Christians in the Europe of his day.[27] In one commentator's eyes,

> The great value of the later Kierkegaard's Christian social-political thought lies, however, finally in clarifying the peculiarly modern forces of idolatry and the subversion of Christianity to worldly norms. In probing the nature of idolatry, Kierkegaard reveals with clarity and passion the ways in which the 'world,' usually in the form of the state, church, or group, and often in the name of Christianity, claims to speak in the name

---

Romanticism'. Karl Barth, 'An Introductory Essay', trans. J.L. Adams, in Ludwig Feuerbach, *The Essence of Christianity*, trans. George Eliot (New York: Harper, 1957), p. xx.

27   See Søren Kierkegaard, *Two Ages: The Age of Revolution and the Present Age: A Literary Review*, eds. and trans. Howard V. Hong and Edna H. Hong (Princeton: Princeton University Press, 1978), p. 91.

of God, whereas it actually merely sacralizes that group's self-interest, whether in the deathlike 'silence' of Golden Age Denmark's elitist amalgamation of Christianity and culture in 'Christendom,' or in the subtle or horrific tyrannies of the modern age. Kierkegaard knew, as surely as did Feuerbach, how 'God' becomes the mere projection of the group's identity and values, in particular how the church sides with the crucifiers. But, unlike, Feuerbach, Kierkegaard saw God as the Holy One who stands with the outcast and crucified. Christ as Pattern for discipleship in this way provides the transcendent revealed model for existence that offers the standard for an individual to stand against her or his culture, to embody and 'do the truth'.[28]

Though there are multiple paths one could take with his work, as the above commentary illustrates, Kierkegaard's stance against the 'horrific tyrannies of the modern age' certainly echoes Barth's opposition to Nazism, something that puts both authors at tremendous odds with Schmitt's defense of Hitler's reign. Despite this connection, however, the language of justification for sovereign-metaphysical forms, though shifting from communal, political endorsement to the individual level, maintains many of the same elements that have yet to be clearly accounted for.[29]

Kierkegaard's strong stance against 'Christendom' meant that he regarded himself as not being a 'Christian' as a citizen of such a community, but rather strove to exist as an exception to every system in order to establish an existential identification with the Christian proclamation. Hence, one can understand his placing stress upon a form of subjectivity that comes across as the ultimate ground or foundation (as what legitimates a sovereign form) through an individual decision often constructed as a 'leap of faith'. This focus (perhaps even overemphasis[30]) upon the individual, existential circumstance of the believer was the result of what Kierkegaard saw as a paradoxical situation in which we find ourselves as humans.[31] Our experience of the 'Absolute' is

---

28   David J. Gouwens, *Kierkegaard as Religious Thinker* (Cambridge: Cambridge University Press, 1996), pp. 231–232.
29   Rebecca Gould, 'Laws, Exceptions, Norms: Kierkegaard, Schmitt, and Benjamin on the Exception', *Telos* 162 (2013), pp. 1–19.
30   See Justo L. González, *A History of Christian Thought, Vol. 3: From the Protestant Reformation to the Twentieth Century* (Nashville, TN: Abingdon Press, 1987), p. 373.
31   In the context of Kierkegaard's thought, González suggests that 'Actual human existence is always involved in paradox and pathos and these are two categories that abstract logic cannot encompass'. González, *A History of Christian Thought, Vol. 3*, p. 367.

always a singular experience, one that can be seen to challenge the ruling, ecclesial structures that be.[32] As such, in Gary Dorrien's words, 'Christianity cares only about subjectivity', and it is only in one's subjectivity that truth can be found.[33] We see such a sentiment echoed years later in the writings of the Lutheran theologian Dietrich Bonhoeffer who would utilize Kierkegaard's insights in conjunction with Barth's theological challenges to liberal theology in order to craft his political and theological opposition to the German Churches of his day that had failed to stand up to Hitler.[34] It also played a role as well in Bonhoeffer's decision to respond with violent action to Hitler's leadership—a point that cannot be easily overlooked.

Kierkegaard's response to what he saw as the philosophically dominant Hegelian 'both/and' was a defiant and decisionistic 'either/or' that labelled everyone refusing to make such a decision as 'spineless'[35]—and this was precisely what would appeal to Barth so many years later as he crafted his systematically-formulated *Church Dogmatics*. The Christian, Barth felt, must take a stand for Christ against the liberal, rationalist tendencies to incorporate everything within itself and so to let every voice be heard—a tendency that would ultimately dilute the truth of Christianity. In sharp contrast to Schmitt, all authorities, from the monarch to religious authorities, all of which were deemed 'make believe' by Kierkegaard, were perceived as unable to match the choice of the individual believer made in solitary faith and dependent upon no one else (again, precisely what Schmitt would relegate exclusively to the position of the sovereign by definition).[36] Moreover, Kierkegaard savaged the abstract

---

32 See González, *A History of Christian Thought, Vol. 3*, p. 371.

33 Gary Dorrien, *Kantian Reason and Hegelian Spirit: The Idealistic Logic of Modern Theology* (Oxford: Wiley-Blackwell, 2015), p. 279.

34 'Kierkegaard stood out from his time by not belonging to it. Liberal theology, believing in reason, historical criticism, and modern cultural progress, was about the wrong things. It let go of any real connection to New Testament Christianity and sought to replace muddled state church orthodoxies that were already hopelessly compromised. Kierkegaard spurned Schleiermacher-style liberalism as a boring and enervated waste of time. He repudiated Hegelianism and his debts to it, except for the parts that he called something else. Had he lived to see the Social Gospel, he would have blasted that too'. Dorrien, *Kantian Reason and Hegelian Spirit*, p. 302.

35 See, among many other passages, how Kierkegaard defends the decision of the either/or in Kierkegaard, *Two Ages*, p. 67.

36 Kierkegaard, *Two Ages*, pp. 80–81. 'We do not want a powerful king any more than we want a liberator or religious authority. No, quite harmlessly and inoffensively we allow the established order to go on, but in a reflective knowledge we are more or less aware of its non-existence' (p. 81).

'public' as much as he critiqued the State and the Church, offering us a glimpse into the power of individual freedom and choice that would come to identify so much of later existentialist thought.[37] His refusal to accept that a liberal society held the key to transforming our world was in turn what fostered a focus on individual autonomy and choice as strong as was Schmitt's reliance upon the decision of the sovereign. As he had described it in his *Two Ages*:

> It is very doubtful, then, that the age will be saved by the idea of sociality, of association. [...] Not until the single individual has established an ethical stance despite the whole world, not until then can there be any question of genuinely uniting; otherwise it gets to be a union of people who separately are weak, a union as unbeautiful and depraved as a child-marriage. Formerly the ruler, the man of excellence, the men of prominence each had his own view; the others were so settled and unquestioning that they did not dare or could not have an opinion. Now everyone can have an opinion, but there must be a lumping together numerically in order to have it.[38]

In a language that would eventually resurface with dramatic force in Heidegger's *Being and Time*, only the individual can rise up above the so-called 'leveling' of abstraction and the demolishing of authority that suffocates the moment of decision and resoluteness for the individual.[39] Yet one must also hesitate to pronounce Kierkegaard's critique of association, or modern liberal-social tendencies as a form of anti-democratic rhetoric (as Schmitt was tempted to do), as its closest sensibility may ultimately be with some form of libertarianism. It is the individual, not the collective, that is capable of rising to greatness through contemporaneity with Christ (what takes place in the moment of a decision for faith), which amounts to little more, in a purely political sense, than making a decision to posit oneself as sovereign.[40]

---

37 Kierkegaard, *Two Ages*, p. 93.
38 Kierkegaard, *Two Ages*, p. 106.
39 Kierkegaard, *Two Ages*, pp. 107–108. See also how the 'moment' develops as a significant concept in this vein of thought in Søren Kierkegaard, *The Moment and Late Writings*, eds. and trans. Howard V. Hong and Edna H. Hong (Princeton: Princeton University Press, 1998).
40 For his discussion of being 'contemporary with Christ' in the context of his critique of Christendom, see Søren Kierkegaard, *Practice in Christianity*, eds. and trans. Howard V. Hong and Edna H. Hong (Princeton: Princeton University Press, 1991).

As the German political theologian Dorothee Soelle would later describe this configuration of the subject, '"Not willing to be oneself" is the desire of weakness, which must capitulate before the superior power of the structures without admitting it. Kierkegaard renders a theological judgment on this man who experiences himself as powerless and entangled—namely, that it is "despair," therefore the antithesis of faith, which determines him'.[41] At the same time, however, Soelle also recognized where the fault-line might be located within his thought by suggesting that 'Kierkegaard analyzes the existential decision that underlies this despair but without examining its social and political origins. In a direct sense, therefore, his category applies to men of another era', much as Kierkegaard himself seemed to suggest in his *Two Ages*.[42] Perhaps the 'sovereign man' of an older era was no longer the modern human being (which has expanded the subject beyond simply men to include women as well), though Kierkegaard found solace and inspiration in nostalgically recalling him. This was a mistake Kierkegaard would not be the last to make.

What becomes clear in all of this at least is that the notion of sovereignty that both Kierkegaard and Schmitt heavily relied upon has been used historically, and frequently, to justify God's existence, though it has also been used to legitimate the state's, and eventually the (mainly Protestant) sovereign self as well.[43] For his part, Schmitt's explicit borrowing of his political-theological vocabulary from Kierkegaard, sans its metaphysical underpinnings, meant that he was able to isolate the political implications of Kierkegaard's thought in order to identify what exactly had been so intriguing about it. Primarily, Schmitt discovered the state of exceptionality that was implicitly linked to the decision and the nature of the sovereign who arose through such an act taking place within a state of exception. In Schmitt's famous phrasing, 'The exception is more interesting than the rule. The rule proves nothing; the exception proves everything: It confirms not only the rule but also its existence, which derives only from the exception'.[44] This state of exception was the proper location for the wholly autonomous sovereign to be found and to establish their rule apart

---

41 Dorothee Soelle, *Political Theology* (Minneapolis, MN: Fortress Press, 1971), p. 95.
42 Soelle, *Political Theology*, p. 95.
43 See the descriptions of this progression in Larry Siedentop, *Inventing the Individual: The Origins of Western Liberalism* (London: Penguin, 2014) and Jean Bethke Elshtain, *Sovereignty: God, State, and Self* (New York: Basic, 2008). Though their conclusions may seem to differ somewhat, as Siedentop champions the critical power of the secular as the child of Western Christianity and Elshtain offers us a 'less than sovereign self', I prefer to read these interpretations together as diagnoses of the same movement, one toward the poverty of the subject in the face of prior metaphysical, sovereign representations.
44 Schmitt, *Political Theology*, p. 15.

from the everyday, (liberal) bureaucratic governance of the people. These very Kierkegaardian formulations make clear how Schmitt's turn to Kierkegaard was essential to determine how 'Sovereign is he who decides on the exception'.[45]

In at least one interpreter's eyes, the sense of political theology that follows for Schmitt '[...] understands authority as decision, links decision to sovereign[ty], and grounds sovereignty in faith. At the foundation is not yet another norm—the ground-norm—but the decision, which always cuts across the is and the ought. It *is* the decision for the *norm*'.[46] As such, the Kierkegaardian emphasis placed upon the moment of decision, or the leap of faith framed as the autonomous choice of the individual toward a faith that will guarantee truth as a form of (sovereign) subjectivity, is enfolded by a notion of paradox that grants the 'mystical foundations of authority' its apparent imprimatur.[47] Such 'mystical foundations' for sovereignty—as the phrase has been used in the works of Jacques Derrida and Pierre Bourdieu alike—are well grounded in what Slavoj Žižek has called in his debates with John Milbank the 'misty use of paradox'.[48] In such alleged uses of paradox, Kierkegaard and Schmitt are aligned in a near perfect symmetry as they seek to legitimate the position of the sovereign who creates norm, law, state, self or people all apparently *ex nihilo*, through their paradoxical position outside of all normative law while also being its ground, at least when seen from the perspective of sovereign power.[49]

The 'endless talk' that defined liberalism's commitment to forms of free speech but that had also avoided the moment of decision (and so of faith, for theologians like Kierkegaard and Barth), as Schmitt phrased it, was borrowed directly from Kierkegaard's desire to cease such 'endless talk' through the exceptional moment, where the individual, as sovereign or even 'dictator' over themselves, makes a decision that cuts through the general, unending discourse or doubt.[50] The one who is capable of knowing what they are

---

45   Schmitt, *Political Theology*, p. 5.
46   Paul W. Kahn, *Political Theology: Four New Chapters on the Concept of Sovereignty* (New York: Columbia University Press, 2012), p. 48.
47   Søren Kierkegaard, *Concluding Unscientific Postscript to Philosophical Fragments*, eds. and trans. Howard V. Hong and Edna H. Hong (Princeton: Princeton University Press, 1992).
48   Slavoj Žižek and John Milbank, *The Monstrosity of Christ: Paradox or Dialectic?*, ed. Creston Davis (Cambridge, MA: MIT Press, 2009).
49   On the link between Schmitt and Heidegger specifically in this context, see Kahn, *Political Theology*, p. 60.
50   See the quote from Kierkegaard's *Repetition*, eds. and trans. Howard V. Hong and Edna H. Hong (Princeton: Princeton University Press, 1983) provided in Schmitt, *Political Theology*, p. 15.

against—i.e. who their enemy is—is the individual capable of deciding or distinguishing who they themselves are—the very definition of the political in Schmitt's work, but also the lynchpin of subjectivity in Kierkegaard's.[51] The 'principle of representation', for Schmitt, was dependent upon the presence of personal authority, what the dictator, monarch or pope exemplified, and what for Kierkegaard had lain entirely in the individual (or 'knight') of faith.[52]

The argument could be made that Schmitt's embracing of Roman Catholicism as a 'complex of opposites', or a *complexio oppositorum* that is decidedly not a Hegelian synthesis of some sort, actually bears a striking affinity to Kierkegaardian notion of paradox. This might be said especially to be the case insofar as both conceptualizations are able to evade the dualistic schemes of representation that otherwise define political interaction (e.g. left/right, liberal/conservative) in order to submit one model of politics/faith that strives to stand alone.[53] It is significant to note that these notions of paradox and *complexio oppositorum* are perhaps similar in many ways to an Augustinian notion of *corpus permixtum* that no doubt pervades such theological gestures and aids any such political theologian in connecting the linkages of sovereignty, necessity, glory and autonomy to that of predestination (or the very principle that grounds monarchical and apostolic forms of succession). For Schmitt, the body of the Church, as with the State, redefines the *corpus permixtum* as a global body that sets one part against another, defining either Church or State against what they are not—the basis of his friend/enemy distinction that defines the operations of the political, even if the Church itself, as with the Incarnation, is internally divided against itself.[54]

There is of course an alternative way to read the notions of paradox, *complexio oppositorum* and even *corpus permixtum* as an internal contradiction that discloses the reality of how sovereignty must always be established in conjunction with the governance of the people, or what Michel Foucault

---

51 Carl Schmitt, *The Concept of the Political*, trans. George Schwab (Chicago: University of Chicago Press, 2007). See also the commentary offered on Schmitt in Mark Lilla, *The Reckless Mind: Intellectuals in Politics* (New York: New York Review of Books, 2016), p. 57.

52 Carl Schmitt, *The Necessity of Politics: An Essay on the Representative Idea in the Church and Modern Europe* (London: Sheed & Ward, 1931), pp. 60–61.

53 Carl Schmitt, *Roman Catholicism and Political Form*, trans. G.L. Ulmen (Santa Barbara, CA: Praeger, 1996), pp. 7–9.

54 Gil Anidjar, however, locates within such Schmittian oppositional forms capable of being deconstructed themselves a breakdown of the friend/enemy division that might yet be capable of turning the enemy into the friend and vice versa. See Gil Anidjar, *The Jew, the Arab: A History of the Enemy* (Stanford: Stanford University Press, 2003).

referred to as the governmentality that always accompanies the exercise of sovereign power.[55] Such too was Ernst Kantorowicz's conclusion concerning the existence of the 'king's two bodies' in medieval political theology, as well as Giorgio Agamben's more recent configuration of the bipolar nature of the anthropological machinery that constructs all forms of modern subjectivity.[56] For Roberto Esposito as well, this dynamic exposes the force of the Two, as he terms it, that has governed political hegemony in the West for centuries, often converting the Trinity effectively into a 'Binity' that relies upon the bipolarity of political apparatuses (sovereignty/governmentality as justified through recourse to God/Jesus) in order to cement and legitimate sovereign power.[57]

For both Kierkegaard and Schmitt, however, the apparent move beyond such dualisms clearly meant making a choice for one side over the other, though effectively (albeit unconsciously) legitimating the existence of the dualistic rubric itself. In this sense, neither Kierkegaard nor Schmitt were really able to move beyond the dualistic framework that inspired both passion and decision in order to legitimate sovereign power; they merely reinforced the bipolarity of western political and theological forms that much further. Despite much recent work to illuminate this dualistic framework for both politics and theology, however, this option has dominated a particular strand of contemporary theology, to be sure, but it has also dominated philosophical discourse through its Heideggerian manifestation.

Martin Heidegger and the Attempt to Overcome Metaphysics
The French philosopher Jean Wahl, who was no stranger to the existentialist tendency to focus on the freedom that makes choice possible, was particularly attuned to the Kierkegaardian influence on Heidegger regarding such matters. His 1932 article on 'Heidegger and Kierkegaard' in fact served to illuminate this intellectual relationship beyond any doubt.[58] His demonstration

---

55   Michel Foucault, *The Birth of Biopolitics: Lectures at the Collège de France, 1978–1979*, ed. Michel Senellart, trans. Graham Burchell (New York: Picador, 2008).
56   Ernst H. Kantorowicz, *The King's Two Bodies: A Study in Medieval Political Theology* (Princeton: Princeton University Press, 2016) and Agamben, *The Use of Bodies*.
57   Esposito, *Two*. See also the critique of western forms of political theology vis-à-vis the Christian critique of them in Erik Peterson, 'Monotheism as a Political Problem: A Contribution to the History of Political Theology in the Roman Empire', *Theological Tractates*, ed. and trans. Michael J. Hollerich (Stanford: Stanford University Press, 2011), pp. 68–105.
58   Jean Wahl, 'Heidegger and Kierkegaard: An Investigation into the Original Elements of Heidegger's Philosophy', *Transcendence and the Concrete: Selected Writings*, eds. Alan D. Schrift and Ian Alexander Moore (New York: Fordham University Press, 2017), pp. 107–131.

of Kierkegaard's influence upon Heidegger's thought was convincing enough that Jean-Paul Sartre had cited Wahl's article in his magnum opus *Being and Nothingness* in order to further cement the connection between these two authors within the context of his own existentialist reflections.⁵⁹ Both authors were so fascinating and helpful to Sartre because his own brand of existentialism would offer a robust defense of the autonomous subject, one mired in a freedom that likewise allowed it to reign as sovereign over itself. And, in many ways, this philosophical-theological temptation has subsequently never receded from view. Even in the face of post-structuralist critiques of the subject today, it is possible to retrieve such a sovereign self, with or without Sartre, in order to bolster the claims of autonomy in defense of certain authorities and communities, as I will highlight in the next part.⁶⁰

Moving beyond the dualistic impasses of politics and of thought that both Kierkegaard and Schmitt had been unable to extract themselves from was Heidegger's explicit aim, specifically something he attempted through the constitution of a people (*Volk*) that somehow differed from one's inauthentic immersion in ('falling prey to') the 'dictatorship' of the They which attempts to 'level down' any decision for authenticity—what Heidegger had termed resoluteness.⁶¹ As we might recall from Kierkegaard, or from Schmitt's work for that matter, for Heidegger the decision made by the individual for the authentic is grounded only in oneself, whether as a singular individual (for Kierkegaard) or as the always singular sovereign (for Schmitt).⁶² On occasion, Heidegger himself even noted what he had learned from Kierkegaard specifically regarding one's capacity to choose oneself in order to formulate the self.⁶³ Inauthenticity, in this sense, comes about as an everyday reality when the They makes the choice for the individual and so it remains indefinite as to who actually does

---

59   Jean-Paul Sartre, *Being and Nothingness*, trans. Hazel E. Barnes (New York: Washington Square, 1956), p. 65.
60   See, among others, Alain Renaut, *The Era of the Individual: A Contribution to a History of Subjectivity*, trans. M.B. DeBovoise and Franklin Philip (Princeton: Princeton University Press, 1997). See also the commentary offered in Noreen Khawaja, *The Religion of Existence: Asceticism in Philosophy from Kierkegaard to Sartre* (Chicago: University of Chicago Press, 2016).
61   Martin Heidegger, *Being and Time*, trans. Joan Stambaugh (Albany, NY: State University of New York Press, 1996), pp. 119, 249.
62   Heidegger, *Being and Time*, p. 137.
63   Martin Heidegger, *The Metaphysical Foundations of Logic*, trans. Michael Heim (Bloomington, IN: Indiana University Press, 1984), pp. 190–191.

the choosing.⁶⁴ Making a decision for one's potentiality of being is rather what constitutes the authentic as a form of resoluteness.⁶⁵

As Heidegger would put forth in his highly influential study *Being and Time*, Da-sein, or the form of existence unique to human beings, is 'familiar to us as the "voice of conscience"', which discloses something to us.⁶⁶ Conscience summons Da-sein 'to its ownmost quality of being a lack', which is to say it forms the sense of guilt within us which is not to be confused with theories of the conscience stemming from the 'soul, understanding, will, or feeling', as in historical theological formulations. The conscience summons one to one's own self, to Da-sein itself through the call of conscience which brings the self to itself, establishing itself as the ground for its own authenticity *as* self—much as what I have been calling the sovereign subject in Kierkegaardian or even Schmittian terms. In Heidegger's phrasing, 'Conscience calls the self of Da-sein forth from its lostness in the they', though, again, the call comes *from* us and yet arises as if from *beyond* us—a state of *being beyond* oneself that brings about the sense of its not yet fully having arrived and which is often mistaken for God. It is also a paradoxical situation wherein the self grounds itself, much as Schmitt had claimed the sovereign legitimates its own power. The sense of resoluteness that appears as a tautological foundation for the self is actually a form of creation *ex nihilo* that grounds the sovereign subject both in itself and through itself—a point that, some years later, Derrida too was quick to define as one of the major characteristics of sovereignty.⁶⁷

As Heidegger will further develop things in a decidedly Kierkegaardian register, 'the Moment', which is the authentic present, establishes a sense of an ec-stasy that is not a 'now'. The Moment is the site of encounter with 'something at hand or objectively present', though he will also add, not every present is in the Moment. 'This ecstasy makes it possible for Da-sein to be able to take over resolutely the being that it already is', establishing the self as subject over itself through recourse to accessing the sense of Being beyond its merely ontic existence. '*The Moment* brings existence to the situation and discloses the authentic "There"'. Resoluteness, as such, brings us back from a state of lostness and so the actual situation, of being toward death, is 'disclosed as the

---

64 Heidegger, *Being and Time*, p. 248.
65 Heidegger, *Being and Time*, p. 249.
66 Heidegger, *Being and Time*, pp. 248–249.
67 Heidegger, *Being and Time*, pp. 248–254. See also Jacques Derrida, *Rogues: Two Essays on Reason*, trans. Pascale-Anne Brault and Michael Naas (Stanford: Stanford University Press, 2005).

held Moment'. Existence, he will continue, can 'master the everyday in the Moment', though it cannot do so forever, but only at times.[68]

What is significant to note in this configuration is that the Moment functions as a decision in a Kierkegaardian sense, or as that which establishes the subject (as *truth*) through the leap undertaken as a Moment of founding the self upon the exceptional.[69] Schmitt had likewise sensed this to be the general (political) implication of Kierkegaard's (theological) thought and so took insight from Kierkegaard's elevation of the subject above the 'they' or the masses of Christendom who prevented an authentic Christian from rising up among them. In *Being and Time*, however, we see Heidegger's authentic resoluteness established in opposition to the 'they-self' and everydayness, though somehow also open to the *Volk* or people who might pass along the destiny of a tradition.

In a very specific sense, I would argue that Heidegger assumes the possibility of overcoming onto-theology and metaphysics, but does not deal with the possibilities embedded in the potential reality of a secularized political theology, as Schmitt does—the very lapse that made him extremely vulnerable to the sovereign-dictatorial form of Nazism without fully realizing, in some ways, that he dwelt in this state. In so many ways, the field of political theology today is only now offering a response to Heidegger's failure in this regard. What we have at least learned from his failure, however, is that onto-theology cannot be overcome purely in existential-phenomenological terms; there must be a political dimension analyzed as well, but not through the one-sided defense that Schmitt had sought to make. Trying to do away with onto-theology once and for all is an attempt to overcome the dualisms inherent within political forms (left/right, friend/enemy, etc.)—something that religion and utopias alike dream of, but which does not actually exist as a possibility in our world (an issue which I will take up directly in the final part).[70]

Heidegger had failed to see the link between Kierkegaard's conception of the Moment and its relation to Schmitt's sovereign decision as well as how the secularization of such theological concepts might be used to construct a wholly destructive political theology. In short, Heidegger's failure to grasp the political

---

68   Heidegger, *Being and Time*, pp. 302–339.
69   It is interesting to note as an alternative to such a configuration of the Moment and of the decision associated with it, the formulation of a 'passive decision' in Geoffrey Bennington's reading of deconstructionism and its attempt to move beyond the mistakes of both Heidegger and Foucault. See Geoffrey Bennington, *Scatter 1: The Politics of Politics in Foucault, Heidegger, and Derrida* (New York: Fordham University Press, 2016).
70   For an elaboration on these political dynamics within any given field of representation, see Ernesto Laclau, *The Rhetorical Foundations of Society* (London: Verso, 2014).

implications of the Moment through the secularization of Kierkegaardian lines of thought (or rather from grasping the political stakes of what was already latent within Kierkegaard's theology) leaves him open to re-creating a metaphysical, political-theological structure of his own, though one that pretends it is not performing a theological operation while it most certainly does.[71] (This is the same failure as well that lingers in its opposite form in those theologians who believe they can perform a theological operation while avoiding a political one, which is likewise impossible.)

How does one begin to trace the lines of the political within a philosophy that strives to eliminate all traces of onto-theology and of all metaphysical presumptions if theology has been identified as being political all along (and as Schmitt clearly saw)? Was this often highly problematic relationship why Heidegger had himself failed to theorize the political? Was this what had misled him politically, and therefore to presume he had left all metaphysics behind and so succumb to the purely ideological? Was this also why Heidegger kept a certain distance from Kierkegaard at the same time as he drew nearer to Kierkegaard's notion of the sovereign subject who makes a decision for faith in the Moment?

For Heidegger, the *Volk* was the only way through the intractable dualism between liberalism and authoritarianism, an effort that makes his relations to National Socialism both a clear temptation and yet highly complicated at the same time.[72] There was certainly present in his thought a critique of tradition, as that which potentially blinded Da-sein from discovering its true ground, at the same time as the heritage of the *Volk* was somehow separately elevated as

---

[71] Walter Benjamin's conception of the 'now-time' (*Jetztzeit*) can be seen as a direct refutation of the Heideggerian-Kierkegaardian 'moment' as in Benjamin's formulation there is no choice made that elevates us above the vulgar conception of the now and of time, but rather a moment that has been repressed appearing within the now itself. The losers of history become fleetingly visible for a moment within the now, thus dividing the present moment and leaving only what Agamben has called the 'time that remains'. In this sense, there is no purely existential-phenomenological sense of time, as it is always infected with a political dimension as well. I would suggest that this is what Heidegger missed in his conceptualizations of time and what allowed both for his philosophy to be a pseudo-theology and for him to be politically misguided by ignoring the political implications of his own thought. See Walter Benjamin, 'On the Concept of History' in Howard Eiland and Michael W. Jennings, eds., *Selected Writings*, vol. 4, trans. Edmund Jephcott et al. (Cambridge, MA: Belknap, 2003).

[72] See James Phillips, *Heidegger's Volk: Between National Socialism and Poetry* (Stanford: Stanford University Press, 2005), pp. 54–55.

an authentic possibility.[73] Heidegger had spoken toward the end of *Being and Time* of the resoluteness with which heritage is handed down, and there is within this analysis an experience of fate in this heritage which calls to mind the Greek epic form and the heroes who were given over to their fate, but held up as resolute in their acceptance of it. This is where he could also suggest that there was a power that comes to one who embraces their powerlessness through freedom, as having 'chosen the choice' made against them—this is destiny. Destiny unfolded consequently as an 'occurrence of the community, of a people' that dwells in fate only through the exercise of 'death, guilt, conscience, freedom, and finitude'. Only through such a realization of one's destiny can one dwell in the Moment. This is where Da-sein 'chooses its heroes' and from whence loyalty is derived. Accepting one's fate in resoluteness consequently frees one from illusion, though, in reality, and here moving beyond Heidegger in order to account for his actions, it may mire one more deeply within it.[74]

Despite such conjectures that remain more than slightly problematic in his thought, there is also a particular irony present in the way by which Heidegger attempts to separate theology from philosophy, and so to attempt to remove metaphysical presumptions from philosophical reflection, in such a way that yet preserves a Barthian distance from the world.[75] This is the same impetus that feigns the removal of all 'worldly' politics from the domain of the theological, but which, as Schmitt foresaw, actually conceals the theological at the heart of the political (and vice versa). For Heidegger faith is considered as a type of rebirth, as an existentiell faith, and as a form of destiny, dealing with what is revealed as disclosed solely through faith. Heidegger's goal for theology is concrete Christian existence, not a 'valid system of theological propositions'. Systematic theology was an attempt to grasp this existence. It was thus a practical science, '[...] not speculative knowledge about God', as such. Systematic theology was not 'the philosophy of religion applied to the Christian religion': 'The conceptuality proper to theology can grow only out of theology itself', a sentiment that precisely mirrors a Barthian trajectory in some ways, and certainly speaks to those theologies that seek to criticize the philosophy of religion as not embodied in some manner—a notion which applies to continental philosophical accounts of religion/Christianity (and its genealogical, negative

---

73   Heidegger, *Being and Time*, pp. 18–19.
74   Heidegger, *Being and Time*, pp. 351–357.
75   Heidegger, 'Phenomenology and Theology', *Pathmarks*, ed. William McNeill (Cambridge: Cambridge University Press, 1998).

political-theological forays) almost entirely.⁷⁶ As he would conclude, 'Rather, theology itself is founded primarily by faith', and, finally going a step further, '[t]he substantive legitimacy of all theological knowledge is grounded in faith itself, originates out of faith, and leaps back into faith'.⁷⁷

Despite his insistence that he was engaged in no such theological speculation himself, Heidegger's ability to re-create the conditions of a Barthian dialectical theology that kept faith utterly distinct from the world was what became a secularized philosophy and an implicit, but never openly, theorized politics. So too had his attempt to keep a certain distance from Kierkegaardian metaphysics become that which precisely left him vulnerable to the same temptations that Schmitt had been more consciously aware of in his political formulations. By disavowing the impulse for a metaphysically generated authoritarian position, Heidegger found himself opening a door toward legitimating the destiny of a heritage, a *Volk*, that somehow appeared to transcend the everydayness of the They.

The truth, contra this Kierkegaardian-Schmittian-Heideggerian line of inquiry, is that we are faced with a 'false dilemma' of having to make a choice between sovereignty and democracy (or liberalism), as the one actually invokes the necessity of the existence of the other.⁷⁸ We simply cannot escape the dualistic polarity between sovereignty and governance, as Foucault, Agamben and Esposito have all described this tension in their overlapping studies of political and theological forms within western thought.⁷⁹ This insight is what has also recently led Paul Kahn, among others, to advocate for the necessity of sovereignty within liberal-democratic societies, as difficult as this idea might sound to those sensitive to authoritarian tendencies within western political forms.⁸⁰

---

76   A very interesting possibility to ground such a critique may be accessed through an inspection of the role of the (human) body itself as a point of undecidability between persons and things. See the argument given in Roberto Esposito, *Persons and Things: From the Body's Point of View*, trans. Zakiya Hanafi (London: Polity, 2015).

77   Heidegger, 'Phenomenology and Theology', pp. 44–50.

78   Dimitris Vardoulakis, *Sovereignty and Its Other: Toward the Dejustification of Violence* (New York: Fordham University Press, 2013), p. 202.

79   See, in particular, the way this subject is explored in Giorgio Agamben, *Homo Sacer: Sovereign Power and Bare Life*, trans. Daniel Heller-Roazen (Stanford: Stanford University Press, 1998).

80   Kahn, *Political Theology* and Paul W. Kahn, *Putting Liberalism in Its Place* (Princeton: Princeton University Press, 2005). One might think here too of the work of Mark Lilla who is frequently criticized by those politically on the left in the United States for his defense of sovereign forms from within a more or less 'liberal' perspective. See Mark Lilla, *The Once and Future Liberal: After Identity Politics* (New York: Harper, 2017).

As we note this necessity, however, the field of polarized (and political) tensions within theology often succumbs to some of these same temptations through its (Barthian) justifications for the Church as autonomous and sovereign alongside virulent critiques of liberal theological forms, as well as through those political theologies today that point toward the insurrectionary power of challenging (neo)liberal society in the name of a radical democracy that can never become a historical, actual state.[81] The political theologies such as we find in Stanley Hauerwas or John Milbank, for example, which insist that the first task of the Church must be to remain the Church performs a tautological imperative that intends to ground the Church in its identity alone—again, the very principle that sought to legitimate sovereign forms according to Schmitt. This Barthian proposition can only illuminate a Church dogmatically intent on establishing its own foundations apart from the world, one that perhaps maintains a postmodern 'simulated relationship to the past' in an attempt to solidify its grounding in an 'origin', as Fredric Jameson has described the theology of John Howard Yoder, for example.[82]

Faithfully and forever accompanying such sovereign theological gestures, however, are those (implicitly 'negative') theologies that would endlessly deconstruct whatever ecclesial form or notion of God presents itself—those characteristically immersed in continental philosophical lines of thought, such as in Jacques Derrida, John Caputo or Gianni Vattimo—and which never arrive at pronouncing exactly what a theology or a Church should contain content-wise in a historical sense. This (hypocritical) impasse from both sides characterizes much of contemporary theology and the continental philosophy of religion alike, as well as their occasional antipathy toward one another, though many are loath to admit the impasse exists in the first place in order to secure their viewpoint against its counterpart in a somewhat Schmittian (friend/enemy) political fashion. The time for mistaking one's enemy *as* one's enemy may perhaps be overcome if we are able to see such an impasse for what it really is: a dualistic split within the reality of all political-theological formulations.

---

81 Carl A. Raschke, *Force of God: Political Theology and the Crisis of Liberal Democracy* (New York: Columbia University Press, 2015). See also Jeffrey W. Robbins, *Radical Democracy and Political Theology* (New York: Columbia University Press, 2011) and Clayton Crockett, *Radical Political Theology: Religion and Politics After Liberalism* (New York: Columbia University Press, 2013).

82 Fredric Jameson, *Postmodernism: Or, the Cultural Logic of Late Capitalism* (Durham, NC: Duke University Press, 1991), pp. 390–391.

Part 2: Reassessing the Dualisms within Political Theology

As I tried to make clear in the previous part, there is an impasse between continental philosophy (especially as embodied in those working within the field of continental philosophy of religion) and confessional theological communities. Moreover, this impasse reflects the political one between the 'endless conversation' or negative deconstructive acts that characterize much of modern liberalism and the sovereign gestures that accompany actually existing communities and churches. Though the tension between these two perspectives is lamentable in many regards, it is also, as it should be, inescapable and so also a productive tension if viewed from the right angle. As I hope to demonstrate in the present part, such a tension will not go away and is discernable in numerous philosophical and theological positions, but might also be more fruitfully elucidated and harnessed for more beneficial ends.

The Well-Founded Fears of Apostasy and Transgression within Continental Philosophy

At the conclusion of Shūsaku Endō's novel *Silence* it is more than just the authenticity of Christian, or at least Jesuit, missionary activity that is called into question.[83] The entirety of Western Christianity is directly interrogated by the same question that has secretly haunted the West for centuries: is the only way to remain faithful to a relationship, in the end, whether religious or otherwise, that of apostasy, of transgressing what had once appeared as an almost sacred bond? As Jacques Derrida has amply demonstrated in his work, perhaps the only authentic gift that one can give is one that is given in secret, so that it does not even appear as a gift, which would otherwise inscribe a person within an economy of relations based on an expectation of reciprocity. To truly give a gift to someone, it must be done in such a way that it does not even appear as a gift and remains therefore undetected by the receiver *as* a gift.[84] Within this act of secretly giving gifts that do not bear the identity of being a gift in the end— which is to say that the truest gift will not appear as a gift, but as a renunciation of the economy of gifting itself—we are forced to reckon with the question that Endo presents us: is the demand to love another person one that involves the renunciation of any accumulated identity that such loving often brings? That is, to love another properly, to genuinely love them, must one be willing to give up their illusions of who they think they are (as a loving person), so that

---

83   Shūsaku Endō, *Silence* (New York: Picador, 2016).
84   Jacques Derrida, *The Gift of Death*, trans. David Wills (Chicago: University of Chicago Press, 1995).

they might reveal a fractured and broken self only, the vulnerability that alone is capable of loving another person, of giving the gift of love?

This is to say, in other words, that one's loving fidelity to another is perhaps most clearly demonstrated through a renunciation of one's accumulated identity, an act that exhibits only the failure to maintain a particular identity and a welcoming of the transgression of the normative as the very means of preserving one's relationship to it. For Derrida, who was born a Jew, this had meant in his lifetime embracing the figure of the Marrano, the Jew 'in secret', whose identity failed in terms of religious representational economies, for both Christians and for Jews, but which perhaps also offered him the chance to exist differently through his work for others (especially excluded others).[85] The only way for Derrida to remain Jewish and simultaneously, following Heidegger, be faithful to his critique of western metaphysics was to be a Jew 'in secret', to 'rightly pass for an atheist', as he had put it, and so to be the 'last Jew' in some sense as well. Such positions were not an attempt to be elusive or annoying—though many took them at times to be both—but rather to be faithful to the logic of identity's secret, which is, in the end, its failure to be (or possess) what it strongly desires to be (or own). Claiming that he was the 'last Jew' while also passing for an atheist did not make Derrida's stance a uniquely hypocritical possibility—it rather revealed the inherent hypocrisy latent within *every* established identification.

To wager that politics is inherently hypocritical, immersed in its own secret deals, is of course not quite what Derrida was speaking of when he gestured toward a gift given in secret, one that effaces its nature as gift entirely. The politician, contrary to this process of near effacement, merely presents one face while knowingly concealing another, simultaneously allowing a political representational economy to maintain its operations. The difference would seem to be something like a boundary that separates politics and religion. Religion, as itself a discourse of truth, has often sought to embody a purer consistency or integrity that defies engaging in political compromise. Whereas the political is a fractured and fracturing domain, one of separations and binary representations, western theology on the whole has sought to be somewhat more singular and united, more orthodox, offering the believer a form of purity that cannot be replicated in the world of political compromise. In many ways, and as I will take up in a moment as it illuminates the operations of political theology on

---

85   See his contributions to Bettina Bergo, Joseph Cohen and Raphael Zagury-Orly, eds., *Judeities: Questions for Jacques Derrida*, trans. Bettina Bergo and Michael B. Smith (New York: Fordham University Press, 2007).

the whole, politics is historically the realm of the Two (as Roberto Esposito has put it) while theology has sought to articulate the One.

The fact that the Two bleeds easily into the One, and that the One frequently legitimates the Two, however, and following from such analyses in the previous part, provides us with another glimpse at western political theology that can only reveal how politics too often seeks (ideologically) to claim a One-ness (through sovereign power) while theology likewise functions in reality as a bipolar political machinery. Both realms are frequently contested by a multiplicity (or Trinity, for some) that exceeds the dualistic tendencies of political representation. Politics, as Bruno Latour makes clear, expects a fracture of the One into Two in order to maintain its façade (e.g. the public/private distinction, discourses on rights as founded in persons established over and against non-persons and so forth), but the religious sits uneasy with such admissions, preferring to recover what is lost in this split for its own ends. Religion therefore has typically sought to recognize itself as the rejection of hypocrisy altogether. But, as Derrida had tried to demonstrate, hypocrisy may not actually escape the religious domain, but the religious may only take hypocrisy to another level altogether.

The genuine rejection of all forms of hypocrisy—what appears to us as the option emanating from the theological side of things—can only fall in one of two directions, but not both simultaneously; this is the purity of heart that wills 'one thing', as Kierkegaard had put it, and which is sought after in either direction. Attempting to go in both directions at once is not just a recipe for disaster; it is the condition of hypocrisy itself. To elevate oneself above the reproach of being hypocritical—something the traditional politician can never in fact do, as Latour demonstrates—means either to attempt a form of moral purity that cannot sustain itself, to present an honesty that must conceal its faults and broken reasoning even from itself (hence it becomes an ever purer ideological stance), *or* it means to concede failure from the start, what we might call the inherent nature of apostasy—to concede that one is and has always been a hypocrite and cannot exist otherwise. The politician, by recognizing the inherently hypocritical nature of their compromises, masks the Two-ness (dualism) of politics by maintaining a necessary unified One-ness when no such One-ness really exists, thus presenting ideology at its most basic level. The religious believer, according to Derrida, proceeds in the opposite direction, confessing the fracture of their One-ness, its genuine non-existence, as the only means by which to transcend the economy of Two-ness (or the realm of representations and political-economic interactions).

In the infinite loneliness of apostasy, one's only consolation comes from a source beyond oneself and beyond the community that recognizes the apostate as such. It comes, then, from God alone, but a God who only appears once the One-ness (of God) has been shattered. The lesson of Endō's novel in many ways is that God is actually *not* silent before the apostate, but actually communicates to the apostate who lacks any community to validate their identity *as* an apostate. For the 'believer' who refuses to embrace the act of loving that will ultimately brand them as an apostate, and so appearing to be the opposite of what they truly are, there is only the agonizing silence of God, a God who at this point actually, and ironically, does not exist for the 'believer'. It is a silence that actually emanates from the hesitations, fears and reversals of the 'believer' themselves. There is only a silence present because the 'believer' who really does not believe, has their recompense already from the community that gives them the identity they desire so badly, an identity that seems to be the very thing that undergirds their faith—the very thing that potentially tempts the genuine believer *as* apostate to remain in their identity *as* a 'true believer' who in fact does not really believe. Whereas the puritanical (religious) fascist rallies the community to affirm the truths which are actually falsehoods and so to reaffirm their status as a 'true believer', the apostate who believes in something beyond this spectacle of belief must embrace the deeper truth that will ultimately be rejected by the same community as false. In no uncertain terms, this state of affairs is nothing less than Jesus' experience of the Jerusalem crowds who embraced him when they could assume who he was and what he was there to do, involving the political nature of the messianic expectations that surrounded him; they shouted for his death—the death of an apostate—however, when he did not live up to the claims of identity thrust upon him. (Much the same reasoning, it should be noted, underlies Girard's analysis of the scapegoat, as previously noted.)

What will always be true is perhaps something like what Endō places in the mouth of the apostate priest who is the only real believer: 'Even now I am the last priest in this land'.[86] In many ways, and especially in light of Derrida's claim that he was 'the last and the least of the Jews', the Christian West is still contemplating the meaning of this dissolution of identity vis-à-vis the existence and potential dissolution of the sovereign subject. It is still contemplating what it means that Jesus functioned as an apostate and unbeliever in relation to the Jewish faith he was raised within, and whose people he was desperately trying to love. Continental philosophy, for the most part, is where such investigations have been most routinely conducted.

---

86   Endō, *Silence*, p. 204.

The 'Endless' Deconstruction of Identity

Derrida's oeuvre is in many ways a focused meditation on the deconstruction of identity. In political form, this deconstruction can be perceived as the loss of a sovereign self—that is, of a self that sought to maintain its autonomy as sovereign over itself, of then a striving for a totalized self (and characterized by Derrida as an ipseity, as a tautological construction). What he made clear was that many oppressive forms of sovereignty have emerged over time: 'the father, the husband, son, or brother, the proprietor, owner, or seignior, indeed the sovereign. Before any sovereignty of the state, of the nation-state, of the monarch, or, in democracy, of the people, ipseity names a principle of legitimate sovereignty, the accredited or recognized supremacy of a power or a force, a *kratos* or a *cracy*'.[87] In this ipseity that returns the self to the self and that legitimates sovereign power, we can locate the explicitly theological element which justifies its rule or dominance through recourse to its uniqueness or singularity—the way by which it is able to determine itself as sovereign, as we saw in the previous part. What we witness at the foundations of sovereignty is an ipseity established as the dominant One that cannot be rivaled, and so reduces everything else to a nameless, endless field of plural and irreconcilable elements. In fact the inability of anything else to rival the One is what authenticates the sovereignty of its Oneness: 'It declares, declares itself by declaring the One and the sovereignty of the One, of the One and Only, above and beyond the dispersion of the plural'.[88] Such a reading of the origins of political theology places Derrida's understanding of the One within a particular lineage of sovereign power: 'This theogonic mythology of sovereignty belongs to, if it does not actually inaugurate, a long cycle of political theology that is at once paternalistic and patriarchal, and thus masculine, in the filiation father-son-brother'.[89]

In related fashion, the German Egyptologist Jan Assmann has shown how the origins of monotheism provide the context for the development of a form of political thought uniquely indebted to these theological foundations, from the reign and suppression of the monotheistic Pharaoh Akhenaton to Moses' formulation of monotheism as a political system with the One as God

---

87   Derrida, *Rogues*, p. 12.
88   Derrida, *Rogues*, p. 16.
89   Derrida, *Rogues*, p. 17. This analysis offered by Derrida finds a parallel formulation in Pierre Bourdieu's profound study of the structures of male dominance. See Pierre Bourdieu, *Masculine Domination*, trans. Richard Nice (Stanford: Stanford University Press, 2001).

established as Pharaoh was once over the Israelites.[90] Though the One-ness of the Israelites' God was a critique of any human aspirations to sovereignty, it was also what enabled humans to mimic the divine, leaving the question of idolatry (being false forms of sovereignty) as a central unresolved political issue within the heart of monotheism. God as sovereign, as Father, as One, and as Man, has dominated the western political-theological landscape for centuries, though it shows some smalls signs today of rescinding its grip upon social, religious and political institutions in our world.

Building upon the monotheistic political theology of the One as Father, Derrida illustrated the easy flow of power from a conceptualization of the One to its heirs, first the son and then all brothers who follow in the son's footsteps. In a direct line of continuity, this lineage that Derrida recognized within a general conception of sovereignty mirrors and also extends the dualism of father-son that Kantorowicz had correctly identified as the basis for medieval political theology and which Schmitt seemed content to resurrect in an only slightly-modified modern form. Political theology, as Kantorowicz saw, has often functioned in its formulations of Christ as king as a legitimation for sovereign power and hence for the European Catholic monarch.[91] Derrida's contribution was merely to document the way in which this dualistic construction is not limited to the father-son relation, but extends itself into every economy ('brotherhood') that legitimates its power by drawing its force from the power of the sovereign father-son relationship. Such linkages as between the father-son-brother receive confirmation, moreover, as I have already mentioned, in Esposito's notion of the Two, which points directly at this dualistic, fractured foundation of political theology, instead of toward something like a Trinitarian formulation which might undo the 'binity' that has at times replaced the Trinity within Christian political thought.[92] The Two, as Esposito considers it, is the truly dominant political force within the West, what the One flows ceaselessly into when producing the Western 'person' as itself a dualistic creation (e.g. the mind/body split). As Agamben has also demonstrated, such a split (such as with the animal/human divide, or with the split of the human being

---

90 Jan Assmann, *Religion and Cultural Memory: Ten Studies*, trans. Rodney Livingstone (Stanford: Stanford University Press, 2006) and *Of God and Gods: Egypt, Israel, and the Rise of Monotheism* (Madison, WI: University of Wisconsin Press, 2008).

91 Ernst H. Kantorowicz, *The King's Two Bodies: A Study in Medieval Political Theology* (Princeton: Princeton University Press, 2016).

92 Esposito, *Two*.

into *zoē/bios*, 'animal life' and 'political life') continues to dominate political and theological representations above all else.[93]

Derrida's challenge to the Schmittian defense of sovereignty that sought to establish a sense of fraternity or 'brotherhood' that flowed directly from the political nexus of father-son relations (easily wedded throughout history to specific Christological paradigms) was to call for a democracy 'uprooted' from these sovereign bonds.[94] Derrida pointed toward a hope for democracy as an eschatological horizon of justice, something that could never actually be historically embodied per se, but which remained a spectral site of critique for any existing historical democracy.

In more of a theological register, Jeffrey Robbins, drawing in part on Derrida's thought, has admirably tried to posit a form of radical democracy beyond the liberalism that Schmitt had critiqued as opposed to sovereign power and its accompanying, and justifying, political theology.[95] He conjectures that a radical democracy must be based upon a negative freedom that constantly and consistently deconstructs the gestures of sovereign power in our world, giving one the impression of being a negative political theology that does not offer much in terms of positive political projects, but which carefully seeks to safeguard the imposition of sovereign power upon the people. Robbins aims for a democracy apart from liberalism, though his insights too somewhat fail to account not only for how, in Derrida's eyes, liberalism and democracy are frequently taken as synonyms, but also how actually existing liberal societies might practically accept such criticism and yet continue to function with existing political institutions.

Despite Robbin's hopes, which I would suggest are not misguided, Derrida too recognized that sovereignty, always a localized, particular norm, and democracy, or the principle that sustains any sense of universality, are inseparable and yet in permanent contradiction with one another.[96] They are two sides to the particular/universal dichotomy that we perpetually bump up against in philosophical thought. In this fashion, and despite his tendency to critique sovereign power at seemingly every turn in his writing,[97] Derrida admitted that

---

93   Agamben, *The Use of Bodies* and *Homo Sacer*.
94   Jacques Derrida, *The Politics of Friendship*, trans. George Collins (London: Verso, 1997), p. 306.
95   Robbins, *Radical Democracy and Political Theology*, p. 184.
96   Derrida, *Rogues*, p. 100.
97   Viewed from this perspective, we might discern a resonance that has frequently gone unnoticed: Derrida's deconstructive acts were not just rhetorically effective; they strove to mimic the opposite of sovereign power. Carl Schmitt's criticisms of liberalism were

there was an irresolvable paradox of sovereign power that resided in the very existence of this tension, at once calling law and democracy into existence, while also displaying a force 'of the strongest' that works against the foundations of democracy.[98] This paradox of sovereign power, which will be taken up under a number of guises—most notably in the existence of language itself—will ultimately be deemed ineradicable from the existence of humanity.

Schmitt's mistake perhaps was that he did not recognize the hermeneutical tensions embedded deep within traditional forms of political theology. As if by definition he seemingly could not, as he was seeking to legitimate a sovereign dictatorship and so could not admit of any necessity for hermeneutical nuance in his efforts to establish a determinately biased reading of the field as a whole. As we have already seen, the sovereign was the figure, always embodied in a particular person, who renders the authoritative decision that grounds any existing legal framework and who alone is capable of declaring a state of exceptionality with regard to the law. Law, or what unifies the existence of the state, cannot legitimate itself—only the sovereign can do this through a decision that brings law into being. All law, in this sense, rests upon the decision of the sovereign who calls the state into being and guarantees its existence over and against the social chaos that circulated prior to sovereign rule. In this sense, the sovereign functions as a secularized God, the source of the miraculous intervention that brought the state and its laws into being in the first place through an act of creation *ex nihilo*.[99]

Schmitt's critique of liberalism was that liberalism itself had failed to consider how sovereign power was necessary for political order, and so had neglected to account for the decisive role of authority that was seemingly always vested within an individual person. By failing to consider this truth, liberalism pinned its hopes upon avoiding the one that could legitimate its own (legal) foundations. Hence, we hear Schmitt frequently critique liberalism in particularly harsh, but nonetheless somewhat realistic tones: 'The essence of liberalism is

---

essentially that it produced an endless conversation, a long digression on the possibility of making a decision, though the decision that only the sovereign could make through the exercise of the will was never in fact taken. This was the very thing that, in turn, I would argue, gave rise to the intricacies of Derrida's style and portrayal of *différance*. The endless deferral of meaning that was engaged through *différance* is the result of a representational freedom that only later led Derrida to consider from a political point of view. In this light, I would argue that Derrida's style of writing, with its almost endless deferrals and lengthy sentences, is already a way of presenting his argument against a certain sovereign-rhetorical power.

98   Derrida, *Rogues*, p. 101.
99   Schmitt, *Political Theology*, p. 36.

negotiation, a cautious half measure, in the hope that the definitive dispute, the decisive bloody battle, can be transformed into a parliamentary debate and permit the decision to be suspended forever in an everlasting conversation'.[100] We can locate here Schmitt's charge that liberalism seeks only to promote itself and its rhetoric, all the while ignoring the necessary decisions that characterize real politics from the sovereign's point of view. His criticisms of democratic liberalism were therefore countered, in his mind, by an anti-modern Catholic monarchism that could never really be resurrected, but which seemed the only option available to this reactionary political theorist who watched western politics of the 20th Century slide toward the dissolution of strong political and religious forms through the apparent dominance of weak and ineffectual liberal-democratic political models. For Schmitt, however, 'Democracy is the expression of a political relativism and a scientific orientation that are liberated from miracles and dogmas and based on human understanding and critical doubt'.[101] They were therefore not worthy attempts to reform, but only to replace with a surer, steadier, stronger hand.

There is no doubt that this is the precise point at which Schmitt became tempted by the dictatorship of Hitler, and Schmitt's own personal and political woes certainly stem from this faulty logic. His elaboration of the fundamental tension between sovereignty and liberalism, however, was really only just beginning to provoke political and legal theorists. Paul Kahn's more recent work is a prime example of such a Schmittian recovery. In essence, and as noted in the last part, Kahn has argued that modern liberal democracy has failed to take notice of its sovereign foundations, shunning the sacrifices that are necessary to sustain one's faith in the nation-state. This political theological sacrificial logic functions to construct the subjects of the state and cannot be neglected through the endless conversations of liberalism that attempt to avoid such necessary acts.[102]

Kahn's reading of Schmitt and the necessity for sovereign power as a critique of modern liberalism echoes, I would claim, those conservative theological voices today who ceaselessly lament, and fear, the secular relativism that appears to dominate postmodern culture and continental, deconstructive philosophy alike. As if by default they frequently turn their attentions to ending, like Schmitt, the 'endless conversation' that characterizes such liberal culture in favor of an exercise of a sovereign will (subjectivity) that makes clear its decision to believe in the divine and to be part of an ecclesial fold. As one political

---

100   Schmitt, *Political Theology*, p. 63.
101   Schmitt, *Political Theology*, p. 42.
102   Kahn, *Political Theology* and *Putting Liberalism in Its Place*.

theologian in this mold has put it: 'This is precisely the failure of the epoch-critical pretensions of postmodernism: resting complacently on the assumption that the postmodern era is *fait accompli*, it fails to bring us to decision'.[103]

It might be helpful at this point merely to recall that things were no less different for Kierkegaard in the 19th Century when he chose to interject the decision of the believer, the great *either/or*, into the center of a modern, sovereign subjectivity in order to save it from the grand Hegelian synthesis that appeared to threaten and subsume it. Schmitt, whose entire formulation of the exception is indebted to Kierkegaardian thought, is no less vigorous in his embrace of this faithful logic 'that no longer allowed of synthesis': 'No medium exists, said Cardinal Newman, between catholicity and atheism. Everyone formulated a big either/or, the rigor of which sounded more like dictatorship than everlasting conversation'.[104]

The Perpetual Political Theological Complaint against the Negativity of Continental Philosophy

> Conceptions of transcendence will no longer be credible to most educated people, who will settle for either a more or less clear immanence-pantheism or a positivist indifference toward any metaphysics.
>
> CARL SCHMITT[105]

Though these words are Schmitt's, they might just as easily have fallen from the lips of a number of contemporary theologians whose emphasis on the decisiveness of the believer and the transcendence of God likewise fail to account for the political implications of holding such views uncritically. The issue that needs to be addressed directly by political theologians of all stripes, however, is the basic, and seemingly ineradicable, political tensions that Schmitt identified: between friend and enemy, but also between sovereignty and liberalism.

---

103   Oliver O'Donovan, *The Desire of the Nations: Rediscovering the Roots of Political Theology* (Cambridge: Cambridge University Press, 1996), p. 284. Viewing O'Donovan's reading of liberalism, we are not surprised, then, to come across a firm critique of liberalism as a 'false posture of transcendence' at the conclusion of his return to pre-modern sources of political theology (p. 274).

104   Schmitt, *Political Theology*, pp. 53–54. Schmitt's critique, like Kierkegaard, is clearly aimed at Hegel, whose synthesis into a 'higher third' through a dialectics of 'both/and' was the modern legitimation of liberal discourse (p. 55).

105   Schmitt, *Political Theology*, p. 50.

The deadlock between sovereignty and liberalism that Schmitt posited is one that cannot simply be swept away, just as it cannot be resolved per se through the establishment of a dictatorship, or a Church with nothing existing external to it of value. It seems to constitute something like the divergence between a presence encountered (of sovereignty) and representation (of liberal politics), perhaps *the* fundamental political issue yet constantly measured and evaluated in modern philosophical (as in Kantian transcendental subjectivity) and theological discourses.[106] Theology, for its part, contains a lengthy history of trying to determine how transcendence and immanence might interact, often covering the political stakes of this tension with a metaphysical mask. Modern philosophy, in related yet distinct fashion, is filled with so many frustrating attempts to find an alternative to this tension, and often with equally frustrating results, just as a Schmittian political theology will be unable to ever fully eradicate the liberalism that it so terribly despises.

Theologically, this ineradicable tension is played out routinely in that certain tendencies point in the direction of both sovereignty and liberalism, often risking the mistaken conclusion that theologians must inevitably decide on one position at the expense of the other. The larger point, however—the hermeneutical one that is mainly neglected—is that sovereignty and liberalism seem to indicate an inextricably wed tension that *cannot be* eradicated. What we find in the majority of positions on political theology, however, seems to point in the opposite direction: that one side, in the end, must dominate over the other. To suggest as much, however, merely reinscribes the Schmittian friend/enemy dichotomy within the field of political theology itself and thereby negates the possibility for critique and nuance that is actually needed in order to discern what is truly at stake in the domains of, and interactions between, politics, philosophy and theology.

My argument is that by neglecting the inherent and ineradicable tensions that constitute the field of operations we consider as political theology—as then a split between the continental philosophy of religion's lines of genealogy-deconstruction and the communitarian theologians—an opportunity is missed to understand the fractured state of contemporary continental philosophy itself which seems primarily and irreducibly shattered into one half of an interlinked dichotomy that mirrors Schmitt's division between sovereignty and liberalism. From one perspective, continental philosophy functions

---

106   See the way this contrast of presentation and representation is addressed in Jacques Derrida, *Of Grammatology*, trans. Gayatri Chakravorty Spivak (Baltimore, MD: Johns Hopkins University Press, 1997).

as the negative foil to theology's positive constructive project. From another angle, one internal to philosophy itself, there is a failure to grasp the political-theological significance of the division between the phenomenological in its quest to inspect our transcendent origins (and which generally does not engage political issues) and the genealogical-deconstructivist (and here I would add critical theorist as well) which remains mired in the immanent search for historical configurations of power in a quest to dismantle all forms of metaphysical sovereignty. The more one is concerned with theology, the more one searches for a source of revelation that must be deduced phenomenologically. The more one departs from the theological, the more one investigates the human institutions that can only be deconstructed genealogically. The hermeneutical position, as I have already alluded to above, is the recognition that such tensions are constitutive of the field and cannot be eradicated. We need both elements at work together. That is, these are actually two sides of the same coin locked in a permanent rivalry.

At the same time this fracture within continental philosophy is reflected in the nascent field of political theology which is ostensibly divided between the (frequently Barthian) communitarians who embrace a certain Schmittian articulation of decisionism (as belief) rooted in a transcendent deity and the insurrectionist (radical), genealogical political theologians for whom only a somewhat Derridean radical democracy might take us beyond the impasses of sovereignty and liberalism, but which, more than anything, repeats the logic of liberalism's immanent claims. Though such characterizations would perhaps be contested by both sides, I am wagering that there is more truth in this dualistic articulation than either camp has been thus far willing to admit. Such an analysis would go a long way as well toward explaining why the communitarians typically do not address the potential pitfalls of a Schmittian form of political theology (whereas the radical political theologians always begin with Schmitt as if by rule) *and* yet why the radical genealogists almost never speak of concrete political or ecclesial forms in their negative, critical formulations (whereas the communitarians begin, as a rule, with the necessity for actual existing relations).

In this sense, political theology constitutes something less than a field in its own right, and more of a critical operation, or series of operations, that helps to explain the structure of a pre-existing, or given, field, discipline, community, tradition or normative identification—including continental philosophy itself. The overlap and ongoing tensions between the various political theologies that I will be addressing in what follows are merely an attempt to re-negotiate the critical import of the field of political theological operations as a process inherent to continental philosophical thought today.

Communitarian Opposition to the Genealogists

When conceived as a discipline in and of itself, as then a field that needs to be established and maintained, political theology often falls headlong into a dualistic representation that mimics Schmitt's dichotomy of sovereignty and liberalism (or law). In explicitly theological terms, we find multiple versions of its analogous formulation: for example, the (traditional) communitarians, who champion the necessity of belief in the divine and the actual structures of the church, in opposition to the (radical) genealogists, who start with the Nietzschean 'death of God' in modernity and seek to perform a negative political theological operation as a permanent critique of existing ecclesial structures.[107] The communitarian position is in fact *defined* against the genealogist, as Alasdair MacIntyre made explicit in his *Three Rival Versions of Moral Enquiry*:

> It is only by belonging to a community systematically engaged in a dialectical enterprise in which the standards are sovereign over the contending parties that one can begin to learn the truth, by first learning the truth about one's own error, not error from this or that point of view but error as such, the shadow cast by truth as such: contradiction in respect of utterance about the virtues.[108]

Essentially, MacIntyre asks: how can the genealogist, taken up in this context specifically under the names of Nietzsche, Foucault and Deleuze specifically (and we might also add Freud, Agamben and Esposito, among others), make claims about the inherent multiplicity of the subject if they have yet to account for the subjects that they themselves are as well, as they manifest themselves historically *as* individuals and authors even? The genealogical inquiry thus, in his eyes, fails to account for the subject who sifts through history (genealogically-archaeologically) searching for 'this or that point of view', but all the while subsisting in error through the refusal to take account of themselves.[109] There must be a sense of the sovereign subject behind their

---

107 This Nietzschean legacy is, of course, not uncomplicated by its own problematics and inconsistencies. See, among others, Peter Poellner, *Nietzsche and Metaphysics* (Oxford: Clarendon Press, 1995).

108 Alasdair MacIntyre, *Three Rival Versions of Moral Enquiry: Encyclopedia, Genealogy, and Tradition* (Notre Dame, IN: University of Notre Dame Press, 1991), p. 200.

109 Cf. the commentary on Nietzsche's genealogical methods in Randall Havas, *Nietzsche's Genealogy: Nihilism and the Will to Knowledge* (Ithaca, NY: Cornell University Press, 1995).

words, though it is one that goes almost wholly neglected behind the façade of the so-called 'death of the author'.[110]

MacIntyre, much as we will see in those theological voices who follow him, relies explicitly upon the notion of sovereignty to ground any articulation of truth in relation to the subject and so concomitantly the revealing of error. There are rival versions of justice and rationality, he is at pains to stress, but the mere existence of multiple versions does not invalidate 'making universal claims from the standpoint of a tradition'.[111] And a tradition, presumably whatever tradition, stands autonomously free and sovereign over itself, left to its own devices, which are hopefully less violent than other traditions, which, for their part, should fade out over time. This last thesis, one that implicitly mirrors Schmitt's formulation of modern political sovereignty (as with the autonomous, sovereign nation-state) is not explicitly stated in MacIntyre's critique of the genealogists, nor typically in the theologians who follow his lead in championing tradition, community and the practice of the virtues, but it seems to be the only logical outcome of rejecting genealogical self-deception regarding the source of one's self: the sovereign, any actually, historically-existent sovereign power must be defended. That such voices rarely take into account the existence and competing claims of *other* sovereign, autonomous traditions (religions or nations, for example) is a problem that frequently returns to haunt the communitarians, and for good reason. As one can rightly note in the post-liberal theology of George Lindbeck, for example, each tradition is a closed linguistic-cultural system, impenetrable and unyielding to the claims of other traditions.[112] This is its strength, one might argue, as well as its biggest weakness.

The risk in ventures such as this, of course, is that one simply repeats the self-referential gestures of sovereign power blind to the dual effects it has upon those both within a given community who are marginalized by such exercises of descriptive power and those external to it who do not exist as such, but who are affected by the sovereign power wielded (and which inherently excludes them) nonetheless. (We must recall here too how basically Foucault's entire oeuvre is devoted to uncovering the stories of those marginalized by such dominant narratives, again, demonstrating how wide the gulf is between these two viewpoints in the eyes of many.) To neglect the Schmittian heritage, or rather

---

110 MacIntyre, *Three Rival Versions of Moral Enquiry*, p. 210.
111 MacIntyre, 'Précis of *Whose Justice? Which Rationality?*', *The MacIntyre Reader*, ed. Kelvin Knight (Notre Dame, IN: University of Notre Dame Press, 1998), p. 108. See also MacIntyre, *Whose Justice? Which Rationality?* (Notre Dame, IN: University of Notre Dame Press, 1989).
112 George Lindbeck, *The Nature of Doctrine* (Philadelphia: Westminster, 1984).

to pretend as if it did not exist and so to replicate its political theology within a particular tradition or community is to potentially exacerbate and expand the most disturbing aspects of sovereign power, especially as such power functions as an internal mechanism of identity regulation.[113] This is a point almost unconsciously embedded and therefore embodied in communitarian justifications of the Church's existence. To my mind, this is what becomes highly problematic in the postliberalism of George Lindbeck and Stanley Hauerwas, for example, who attempt to move beyond the liberalism that Schmitt too had been so critical of in order to champion a communitarianism that does not recognize the other who exists outside the Church's cultural-linguistic establishment of itself—the sovereign subjectivity of the community's identity.

In this formulation of things there is a necessary lingering affinity with Kierkegaard's political-theological attempts to critique Christendom through his dependence upon the truth of subjectivity itself, a sovereign self that comes into being through a moment of decision—a point that Barth himself once found very appealing, and which frequently seems to undergird communitarian attempts at legitimating a sovereign vision of the Church.[114] Kierkegaard was adamantly opposed to the operations of the political sphere, rather turning toward the sovereignty of the subject who alone could resist it. As we saw in the last part, what we find in Kierkegaard, as in Protestantism in general, is a temptation toward a form of sovereignty that refuses its external claims to political power, while manifesting them internally for itself. Lest this remain a critique of Protestant values alone, I think we see something similar in Cardinal Ratzinger's (Pope Benedict XVI's) efforts to shore up the faithful remnant of Catholicism in an increasingly secularized European context, as much as we see it in ancient Israel's desperate grasps for self-legitimation after the first Temple was destroyed. It is in such contexts of weakness, where the concrete fear is a loss of religious identity and tradition that the desire for autonomous, political sovereignty dominates whatever other urges toward

---

113   Elizabeth Phillips, for example, in her *Political Theology: A Guide for the Perplexed* (London: T&T Clark, 2012), explicitly states that she will leave out the Schmittian heritage in order to focus on the more communitarian side of contemporary political theology.

114   One might note here the use made of Kierkegaard's thought vis-à-vis 'poststructuralist writing' in John Milbank's essay 'The Sublime in Kierkegaard', *Post-Secular Philosophy: Between Philosophy and Theology*, ed. Phillip Blond (London: Routledge, 1998), pp. 131–156. It is interesting too that figures such as Milbank often invoke Kierkegaard, but rarely draw the connection between Kierkegaard, a communitarian defense of the ecclesial structures and Schmitt's political theology.

divesting oneself of such power had existed within the complex and contested philosophies of a given tradition.

At the same time as this legitimation of the sovereign subjectivity of the Church becomes more pronounced, Hauerwas' call to non-violence, in particular, is something that puts him as a communitarian potentially at odds with sovereign power's claims and relationship to violence in general. A possible fracture is thereby opened up within the communitarian view that points toward its relationship with a liberalism that cannot be ignored as somehow also constitutive of the community. In short, Hauerwas yet forces us to contemplate a nuanced understanding of how the community confesses its relation to violence *ad intra* in terms of how the Church is violent towards its own members, but also *ad extra* as the Church faces a violent world outside. I think he spends a good deal of time in his work addressing the issue of violence because such a tension will not go away when the predominant task he faces is to articulate a vision of communal identity that is sovereign and struggles to recognize the sovereignty of other communities (other religious traditions). Hence the political rhetorical effect of proclaiming, as he often does, that the first task of the Church is to be the Church—a tautological paradox that is one of the hallmark statements of sovereign power—implies a certain violence of identity formation that must be accounted for. For as much as he criticizes American political, national claims to sovereignty, his vision of the Church adopts the same acknowledgement of sovereign power when it recognizes the autonomous sovereignty of other religious traditions as well as its own.

The claim often made by Hauerwas that he simply does not know about other religious traditions, which do not have an effect upon his Christian beliefs, is precisely a claim of sovereignty and it is apiece with his critique of a liberal society that refuses to make the unfashionable decision to believe in the God incarnate in Jesus Christ, preferring rather to stew in a potentially relativistic soup that endlessly discusses spirituality without committing to a particular religious tradition. In general, Hauerwas seems to be firmly rooted in a communitarian-sovereign articulation while also recognizing that a non-violent stance implies a critique of these very roots—hence his opposition to certain forms of American imperialism—but I think as well that much remains unresolved in his work, and for reasons such as I have already named.

What seems clear at least is that the most proper home for something like the Schmittian defense of the need for sovereignty is fittingly rooted in a theological context that seeks to legitimate both belief and a transcendent deity. The institution that is church—yet also parallel in its declarations of autonomous sovereignty to the nation-state—can only be made legitimate on such grounds. The aversion to continental philosophy that many within this camp maintain, makes sense from this angle, as it is such voices of deconstruction and genealogical-critical inquiry that threaten to plunge existing ecclesial structures (but all socially normative relations really) into a thick morass of relativism. Maintaining a trenchant *critique of* continental philosophy therefore becomes just as essential for the communitarians as it is essential for the genealogists to embrace whatever latest trends emanate from philosophers working in France, Germany and Italy.

The Other Side of Things

The other side of this perceived dualistic impasse—the negative political theologies that wholly embrace continental philosophy—has tried to acknowledge how it has reached its own limits, the limits of liberalism even (and which seems to be the natural outgrowth of the modern liberal ideal of searching endlessly for more freedom in all things), but also how it cannot risk falling back into an ontotheological, sovereign form. The focus on Nietzschean genealogical methods to upend a given representation—often taken to be violent, oppressive or destructive of individual freedom in some sense—has been envisioned as the task of late modern critical analysis. Figures as diverse as Freud, Foucault, Deleuze and Agamben have all adapted the genealogical approach in an attempt to de-stabilize the sovereign subject seen as the bearer of oppressive forms. The deconstructivist project, incarnated in the work of Derrida, Paul de Man, Jean-Luc Nancy and Simon Critchley, among others, has likewise followed suit in the de-stabilization of identity, though there have been contentious moments between genealogy and deconstructionism to be sure.

Freud, Foucault and Agamben have all been roundly criticized by Derrida as manifesting a form of 'archive fever' in their possible quest for unlocatable origins, though I am not sure that this criticism entirely applies to their methods which seem satisfied at points to merely de-stabilize normative historical representations.[115] In turn, I am also not convinced that Derrida himself fully escapes the same problematic the genealogists are enmeshed within, which is the (also deconstructive) quest to escape every effort made toward being sovereign. Indeed, as I have noted elsewhere, Derrida and Agamben, for example, seem to ceaselessly hurl the charge of attempting to be sovereign at each other over and over again, and both make damning cases for the other's role as sovereign

---

115 Jacques Derrida, *Archive Fever: A Freudian Impression*, trans. Eric Prenowitz (Chicago: University of Chicago Press, 1996). See too the methodological essays by Friedrich Nietzsche, *The Genealogy of Morals*, trans. Walter Kaufmann and R.J. Hollingdale (New York: Vintage, 1989), and by Michel Foucault, 'Nietzsche, Genealogy, History', *The Foucault Reader*, ed. Paul Rabinow (New York: Pantheon, 1984).

author (essentially because no author can escape making a pact with some form of the sovereign self, as MacIntyre rightly noted).[116]

What seems to remain true within the work of each of these genealogist-deconstructionists is that they search for something that exceeds the system of representations and which cannot be pinned down or defined—the essential elements that the communitarians seek to defend. We see this clearly in Derrida's discussion of the possibility for a form of justice that exceeds any legal or representational framework—indeed, justice is defined by its always exceeding the limits of whatever structure or system grants us meaning, or the framework through which we understand any representation. It is perhaps the quest for a space outside of any structure, institutional identity or communal norm, the space wherein critical thought might be exercised and so the possibility of freedom restored when things have drifted too far towards an oppressive, systematic imposition. Theologically, we see such reflections on display in the writings of John Caputo, Richard Kearney, Clayton Crockett, Jeffrey Robbins and Carl Raschke, among others.[117]

I am not fully convinced, however, that we can simply champion a form of radical democracy that exceeds the boundaries of the dualistic field of representations that would see every political split manifest in either a sovereign form of power that is complicit with (onto-theological) notions of the sacred or the endless conversations of liberalism that inevitably trumpet the secular sphere. To claim that one can transcend liberalism through more democracy, such as Robbins and Crockett have recently done, certainly has its merits and should be lauded as a an implicit goal of political theological operations, but I am less certain that it leads to the death of the sovereign or the real God than that it leads to the death of certain historical perceptions of God or of particular, historical sovereigns (who will be reborn in other forms to be sure). Even the mystical traditions, for their part, seem content to recognize this point over and again as the death of one's vision of God can lead to nothing less than a new perception of the divine (which will then itself be destroyed later on, endlessly repeating the cycle). It is for this reason that the ongoing critique of a sovereign form of God will necessarily go hand-in-hand with an uneasy relationship with existing historical political and ecclesial structures. We see

---

116 See my *Between the Canon and the Messiah*.
117 As I have already cited some of the works by Caputo, Crockett, Robbins and Raschke, I would only add Richard Kearney, *The God Who May Be: A Hermeneutics of Religion* (Indianapolis, IN: Indiana University Press, 2001), as well as his *Anatheism: Returning to God After God* (New York: Columbia University Press, 2010).

this in the writings of the poet Christian Wiman as much as in the works of Kearney or Caputo.[118]

Caputo's work, in particular, which strives to follow Derrida somewhat faithfully, is one that seems intent on permanently 'subverting the norm' of ecclesial order, of reinventing the Reformation again and again, and thereby of attempting to let go entirely of the ontotheological God who was the lynchpin of the political theology that Schmitt had sought to resurrect in the modern era. Caputo's resolute pointing toward a God who *insists* rather than commands or *exists* per se is an effort to evolve toward the spiritual (and so the outgrowth of the liberal) but not religious (the remainder of sovereign power), and to champion something like the postmodern reading of a democracy forever still 'to come' as it grows out of the feigned death of a secular liberalism.[119]

Yet I want to ask: are these efforts toward formulating a radical political theology merely shades of the same negative dialectic that had once animated Jürgen Moltmann's vision of the crucified God?[120] Where does the content come from after the deconstruction of a previously existing structure or tradition is performed, if not from some more or less sovereign articulation? This was the question most often put to Derrida amidst the rising charges that he too lacked any sort of political commitment that so obviously was needed (but which also marked his detractors as caught up in a rhetoric grasping at the heels of sovereign power).[121] These questions circulate too around another issue: to what degree does the apparent 'going beyond' of liberalism signal not just the limits of a self-referential liberalism, but a return to sovereignty as well?

Slavoj Žižek's recent criticisms of Agamben's genealogical pursuits parallel these reflections when he suggests that Agamben's efforts to eradicate the divine altogether through an act of absolute profanation (or what he also calls an absolute immanence, or return to a realm of pure potentiality) really return us to the zero ground of where the sacred might be discernable in the first place,

---

118   Christian Wiman, *My Bright Abyss: Meditations of a Modern Believer* (New York: Farrar, Straus and Giroux, 2014).

119   See Caputo, *The Insistence of God*. On the attempts to overcome ontotheology in continental thought in general, see Joeri Schrijvers, *Ontotheological Turnings? The Decentering of the Modern Subject in Recent French Phenomenology* (Albany, NY: State University of New York Press, 2012).

120   Jürgen Moltmann, *The Crucified God: The Cross of Christ as the Foundation and Criticism of Christian Theology*, trans. R.A. Wilson and John Bowden (Minneapolis, MN: Fortress Press, 1993).

121   I discuss this issue more in-depth in 'Slavoj Žižek on Jacques Derrida, or On Derrida's Search for a Middle Ground Between Marx and Benjamin, and his finding Žižek instead', *Philosophy Today* 59:2 (2015) 291–304.

hinting at the restoration of a sovereign self that had otherwise been anathema to the genealogists.[122] Lest this critique should come as a surprise, there seems to be some truth lingering in this assessment that resonates a good deal with the Gospel account of the death of God in the form of Jesus, whose death tore the curtain that separated the holiest of places on earth according to Judaism, thus rendering all sacred space as profane, but also making the divine accessible in a new way at the same time. The larger question, however, is whether exceeding the boundaries of the liberal, rational, secular sphere returns us to contemplate the ways in which sovereign power is permanently embedded in our world and our sense of self.

Perhaps what is needed, from a theological perspective at least, is to recognize the need for both unity (the communitarian perspective) and plurality (the genealogist one), as David Tracy once pleaded.[123] Perhaps also what is needed is more discernment of the differences between the sovereignty of God and the sovereignty of the Christian religion which are often mistakenly confused with one another, as H. Richard Niebuhr pointed out some time ago. In his words,

> To substitute the sovereignty of Christian religion for the sovereignty of the God of Christian faith, though it be done by means of the revelation idea, is to fall into a new type of idolatry, to abandon the standpoint of Christian faith and revelation which are directed toward the God of Jesus Christ and to take the standpoint of a faith directed toward religion or revelation. A revelation that can be used to undergird the claim of Christian faith to universal empire over the souls of men must be something else than the revelation of the God of that Jesus Christ who in faith emptied himself, made himself of no reputation and refused to claim the kingly crown.[124]

This position on the inherent poverty of the Church is what will prompt Niebuhr to claim that theology must be confessional and communitarian, while at the same time admitting its failures and its poverty to be what it

---

122 Žižek, *Less Than Nothing*, p. 987. See also Giorgio Agamben, *Profanations*, trans. Jeff Fort (New York: Zone, 2007).

123 David Tracy, *Blessed Rage for Order: The New Pluralism in Theology* (Chicago: University of Chicago Press, 1996).

124 H. Richard Niebuhr, *The Meaning of Revelation* (Louisville, KY: Westminster John Knox, 2006), pp. 20–21.

wishes itself to be.[125] Perhaps in this wisdom that recognizes the necessity for both sides in the formation of any (religious) identity is a critical narrative waiting to be more fully explored on the reconciliation of sovereignty and liberalism, or the communitarian and the genealogist, the traditionalist and the radical apostate. (Some may rightly argue too that this was what Kierkegaard and Barth, in their own ways, were really after all along.)

If there is any way for political theology to bring together the dualistically structured field of continental thought today it is perhaps by recognizing, as Christina Gschwandtner has, that the field as a whole seems to share an affinity in its fascination with transgressing received boundaries, pushing the limits of human experience to inspect where they lie and noting how they might be re-aligned from what we had previously taken them to measure and demarcate. The fascination with hyperbole, excess and metaphor in continental thought, which inevitably leads its varied conversations toward the domain of the religious, seems to indicate as much.[126] To ask the question of who sets the borders—of revelation, canonical forms, the human/animal division, sovereignty and liberal discussion, male and female—is to ask about how it has been (sovereignly and decisively) defined. To ask about this definition is really another way of asking about who makes the decision about where the boundaries are located, which is to question the (ontotheological) sovereign power who draws the boundaries, but also to reinscribe us within Schmitt's definition of sovereign power once again. From this perspective, there is a reason why continental thought cannot escape the repetitious question of whether we can truly, ever 'overcome ontotheology'.[127] We will need our phenomenologists and communitarians as much as we need our genealogists and deconstructionists, as they represent two halves to a (dualistic) matrix of representations that we have constructed for ourselves.

Lacking an understanding of this performative politics, those working in the field of political theology often fail to grasp how the establishment of different sub-fields within political theology perhaps misses the larger point: that political theology is not a fixed set of opposing camps (e.g. a defense of sovereign power versus liberalism, or communitarianism versus radically democratic insurrectionists), but an exercise of ideological and rhetorical measures designed

---

125   Such a reading of poverty converges with Johann Baptist Metz's account given in his essay *Poverty of Spirit*, trans. John Drury (New York: Paulist Press, 1968).
126   Christina M. Gschwandtner, *Postmodern Apologetics? Arguments for God in Contemporary Philosophy* (New York: Fordham University Press, 2012), p. 292.
127   See, among others, Merold Westphal, *Overcoming Onto-theology: Toward a Postmodern Christian Faith* (New York: Fordham University Press, 2001).

to reinforce either an analogous reasoning process and the institutional or normative structures it legitimates *or* a metaphorical language of excess and hyperbole intended to deconstruct or transgress such identitarian thought.[128] Though this dualistic logic may seem to simply reinscribe us back within the opposing camps of political theology, my hope is that it is more a recognition that such forces are inscribed within every institution, indeed, within every person, or personal identity and narrative, and so are capable of functioning in either direction, even in contradictory fashion. These forces, much as Derrida made central to his project of deconstruction, traverse myriad domains, from the political to the religious, the philosophical to the literary, the economic to the psychological-autobiographical.

Examining the forces and operations of political theology is therefore not the same thing as arguing for a particular representation of the field and so to simply side with or recreate one half of the seemingly permanent fracture between so many 'political theologians'. I do not as such wish to present my analysis as an argument for one side over the other. I want rather to indicate something like the necessity for reconsidering the role of dualistic thinking within theological thought on the whole, something that continental philosophy has been deeply mired in throughout its existence, but which it has had a difficult time explicitly admitting its indebtedness to. My hope is that, by bringing the dualistic impasse within political theology to the fore of continental philosophical thought (or, alternatively, the dualistic impasse within continental philosophy to the fore of political-theological thought), we might be able to access a path for thought itself that enables us to see the larger picture of why such tensions exist in the first place and what we might finally be able to do about them.

Part 3: Continental Thought beyond Dualistic Thinking

The late 20th Century decline in a truly *systematic* theology, often proclaimed as its death, is really, if one can see it from another angle, a revelation of certain political elements at the core of the theological field that have, in the course

---

128 The political contestations of both sides in this struggle to define and maintain a field of academic discourse, especially through the rhetorical and ideological use of dualistic conceptualizations, reflects the sociological analysis of philosophical traditions in Randall Collins, *The Sociology of Philosophies: A Global Theory of Intellectual Change* (Cambridge, MA: Belknap Press, 1998). See also the use of dualistic thinking in the sociological study of modernity given in Anthony Giddens, *Modernity and Self-Identity: Self and Society in the Late Modern Age* (Stanford: Stanford University Press, 1991).

of late modernity, finally been shown to dictate the development and usage of particular political-theological concepts. As I have already shown, no theology is capable of presenting itself shorn of its political implications and vice versa. Political-theological elements, when functioning unrecognized within a given ideological-theological perspective have been detrimental to the practice of theology as well as to the propagation of faith on the whole. The death of systematic theology is thus also capable of being perceived as an opening toward political, economic, social and contextual theologies far more complex than any singular systematic theology could ever be.

One such way in which theology has politicized itself without being conscious of its political impact is through its usage of dualistic concepts that, rather than aid in the dismantling of oppressive power structures, have served to reinforce the normative status quo in the West, generally-speaking. In this final part, I want to focus on those trends in continental thought that pursue models that bring together the two sides of political theology already delineated—the sovereign (communitarian) and the liberal (genealogical-deconstructivist). I will specifically take a look at the two steps that constitute a more proper inspection of these political theological concepts vis-à-vis continental thought: first, through a look at the history and usage of dualisms in western theological thought, before, second, turning to the development of a critical, nondualistic theology that takes seriously the complexity and inherently comparative nature of theological reflection in such a way as to reopen theological thought toward already established continental philosophical insights. In this second vein, I want to focus in conclusion on the ways in which continental phenomenological methods and insights speak directly to the overcoming of dualistic thinking in order to present an alternate vision for the future of continental philosophy and theology.

Representative Dichotomies or Antinomies of Thought

I first note, for example, the ways in which theology has already incorporated certain dualistic structures of thought in the modern period, including the Schmittian distinction between friend and enemy (or the 'saved' and the 'damned') that is said to lie at the base of all political theology. This dualism could also be described as the 'Mosaic' distinction between pure and impure that supports the foundations of monotheism, as in Assmann's work, and the division between the natural and supernatural which undergirds all modern efforts to think the realm of the religious.[129] Indeed, these three demonstrative

---

129   Henri de Lubac, *The Mystery of the Supernatural* (New York: Crossroads, 1998), as well as John Milbank *The Suspended Middle: Henri de Lubac and the Renewed Spirit in Modern Catholic Theology* (Grand Rapids, MI: Eerdmans, 2014).

exemplars are only the beginning of a larger series of interwoven dualisms that have structured the history of theology since its inception, but which have become heightened measures of theological relevance in the modern period: transcendence and immanence, heaven and hell, icon and idol, sacrament and fetish-object, grace and nature, infinite and finite, actuality and potentiality, necessity and contingency, materiality and immateriality, sameness and difference, mind and body, *kataphatic* and *apophatic*, along with omnipotence and weak thought, just to name some of the more pronounced ones that run on occasion like bright threads through the tapestry of continental philosophy as well.

If we were to collect such dualisms into an identifiable listing of how such tensions generate the field of philosophical and theological representations—and especially as such tensions are often played out between communitarian theologians and continental philosophers of religion—we might come up with something akin to the following table:

Particularity	Universality
Love	Justice
Identity	De-centered
Historical	Ahistorical/conceptual
Embodied	Abstract ('buffered')
Communitarian	Globalized
Autonomy	Heteronomy
Authority	Interdependent
Will	Reason
Revelation/faith	Argumentation/plurality of discourses
Sovereignty	Constitutional forms/democracy (governmentality)
Sacrifice	Non-sacrificial
Exceptionality ('state of emergency')	Holistic
Miraculous	No exceptions
Religious (*post*-secular, metaphysical)	Secular
Unilateral action ('decision')	Dialogue ('endless conversation')
Divergence	Convergence
Exclusive (sameness)	Inclusive (difference and diversity)
Coherence (of private, familial lives)	Incoherence (of public discourse)
Homogenous	Heterogeneous
Monarchical/dictatorial (*post*-liberal)	Liberalism ('anarchy')

Infallibility	Fallible
Foundational	Legal system/code
Revolutionary	Reformist/Bureaucratic
Grace/Gospel	Law (sin)
Either/or (Kierkegaard)	Both/and (Hegel)
Analogy (of being) (ontological)	Metaphor/fiction (genealogical)
Creation *ex nihilo*	Working with what is already given
Actuality (God as *purus actus*)	Potentiality
Fact	Legal norms
Necessity	Contingency
Natural law	Artificiality
Authentic experience	Theory of politics
Ultimate meaning	Reasonable discourse
Presentation ('as such')	Representation ('as if')
Transcendence	Immanence
Omnipotent/Strong	Weak ('weak thought')
'Impenetrable'/Unaffected	Vulnerable/Affected
Glory/Majesty	Disgrace/Shame
Providence/Predestination	Free will
Freedom	Fetish
Icon	Idol
Grace	Nature
Revealed	Natural
Law/Rules/Norms	Exceptions/Forms of life
Canons	Messianic forces
Heaven	Earth
Cosmos (order)	*Chaos* (dis-order)
Male	Female
Subject	Object
Master	Slave
Infinite	Finite
Omniscient	Limited knowledge
Immaterial	Material
Mind	Body
Sameness	Difference
Familiar/Friend	Foreign/Enemy
Good/Truth	Evil/Deceptive
Totality	Separate groupings respected
Identity	Non-identifiable

(cont.)

Violence	Non-violence
Duty	Responsibility
Boundaries/Borders	Porous
Positive (theology)/*Kataphatic*	Negative (theology)/*Apophatic*
What can be said	What cannot be said
'From above'	'From below'

Though this chart is certainly not exhaustive, it provides a general sense of how these polarized dichotomies are necessary, and utilized, for a shared intelligibility and the existence of language, as they helpfully demarcate the extremes of what is considered representable. That is, and as it is frequently politicized in a right/left political dualism, we typically understand one another by the position (and identity) taken up vis-à-vis one of these extremes. As has been pointed out in the context of Antonio Gramsci's notion of *senso comune*, or 'common sense' (which also contains the meaning a 'sense' given by the community), dichotomous logics fundamentally ground the left/right dualisms that structures global political interaction, as well as numerous sociological and anthropological theories on human interaction and communication.[130] Quite simply, we use dualistic frameworks of thought in order to navigate our world and to make ourselves socially and linguistically intelligible to one another.

What is noteworthy as well is that such dualisms not only provide the backdrop for making politics, economics, culture, philosophy and aesthetics intelligible, but they also structure the field of theological representations. Theological discourse pivots upon these distinctions, as well as the interconnections made

---

130 See George Hoare and Nathan Sperber, *An Introduction to Antonio Gramsci: His Life, Thought and Legacy* (London: Bloomsbury, 2016), pp. 141–170. Their dualistic framework extends to include, based on David Crow's *Left to Right: The Cultural Shift from Words to Pictures* (London: Thames and Hudson, 2006), a chart incorporating word/image, male/female, verbal/non-verbal, analytical/holistic, Adam/Eve, Apollo/Dionysus, Yang/Yin and so on. They also cite Rodney Needham, ed., *Right and Left: Essays in Dual Symbolic Classification* (Chicago: University of Chicago Press, 1973), which expands their list to include: poverty/wealth, impurity/purity, mystical office/political rank, illegitimacy/legitimacy, nature/culture, disorder/order and anomalous/classified, among others. I would also note the resonance between such dichotomous logics and Pierre Bourdieu's analysis in his *Masculine Domination*.

by those concepts sharing a common side. That is, particular contrasts are historically and creatively often flipped from a particular alignment with a series of dichotomies to the 'other side' so that a new 'paradigm' of thought can emerge, one often charged with deep political and economic consequences.[131] Assessing these various dichotomies likewise opens up to understanding what political stakes are present in contemplating the impact of the field of theology as a whole. This is what one must conclude once they realize that there are theologies that take up a particular (hierarchical) position over another one, and this tension reveals a very active (at times terrifyingly real) political tension between divergent churches/communities (e.g. in more conservative churches that seek to justify the status quo and systemic oppression through recourse to a predestined, 'necessary' plan instituted by a sovereign deity who legitimates male dominance, closed borders and a homogenous culture). There is a political theology implicitly at work in such dualities, one that could also be said to underlie the very real political domains of *this* world. One need only glimpse the long history of religious wars (in European history, for example) and their basis in differing theological positions (i.e. post-Reformation struggles to define the 'presence' actually present in the Eucharist, etc.) to grasp the concrete implications of such dualistic ways of ordering the world.

What we see unfold within the West's theological usage of such dualisms only further cements the political significance of dualisms, and we can note as well how some of the greatest accomplishments in the field are achieved precisely when any particular duality is re-aligned, or any of its terms are shifted, in relation to another series of dualities. When Thomas Aquinas describes God as 'immaterial' and yet as the 'Pure Act' (pure actuality), for example, dividing a more traditional, ancient linkage between immateriality and potentiality, a new paradigm in theology could be said to open up in the West, one that was utilized for centuries to justify God's sovereignty. Likewise, when Martin Luther divides theology into 'theologies of glory' and 'theologies of the cross'; or when nature is aligned with (sovereign) law (e.g. social contract theory) and grace becomes an immanent phenomenon instead of transcendently given; or when certain theologies frame God as being 'our closest friend' *or* the One who remains 'entirely Other', always foreign to us; or as when Emmanuel Levinas chose to contrast totality and infinity;[132] or when we see faith as necessary ('we are restless until we rest in You, O Lord', as in Saint Augustine) or as contingent (God is fine with our not believing, as long as we are moral beings); or, more

---

131 See the general analysis offered in Collins, *The Sociology of Philosophies*.
132 Emmanuel Levinas, *Totality and Infinity: An Essay on Exteriority*, trans. Alphonso Lingis (Pittsburgh, PA: Duquesne University Press, 1969).

recently, when Theodor Adorno and Bruno Latour both chose to collapse subject and object into the same material phenomenon.[133] In each instance something like a potentially new theological paradigm is rendered possible (though not every path is of course historically taken either). In other words, not only is the implementation of dualisms a political occurrence, but every time a theologian reconceives a particular duality in relation to other, already established dualities, we witness the possibility of a paradigm shift in theological thought that may have a tremendous impact upon our understanding of the divine and humanity alike. Though a critical inquiry into the use of dualisms and their political impact in this context has not been significantly undertaken at present, I want to render more transparent the processes that make dualisms central to theological discourse because I believe it will help illuminate the impasse between theology and continental philosophy, as I have already suggested.

This suggestion is also made in order to state that often western theologies in reality say very little (if at times *anything*) about the existence and nature of the divine; they are rather often statements about *our* own existence and nature, the very foundations of how we try to describe and articulate *our* being. Problems arise when we forget our own involvement in the various representations we create, and when we, as humans, assume that the representation is an actual presentation of the divine itself (the 'thing itself' that we search after, but cannot seem to locate). For example, how many of those characteristics that appear to sit on the border between the divine and the human could just as accurately be used to define the border between the human and the 'animal'—a subject much commented upon by continental philosophers intrigued by sovereignty?[134] And what does this say about our 'essence' and how we seek to legitimate it?

For example, theologians have historically often claimed that God is sovereign over our world, and that such a position somehow legitimates the sovereignty of the king—a typical medieval political theological construction. What we fail to think about is whether or not our vision of God's sovereignty is in fact our own human conception of a very worldly sovereign power that has been placed upon a deity who might actually have little to do with it. As Pierre Manent has put it, humanity created sovereignty as a concept that put it

---

133   Theodor W. Adorno, *Negative Dialectics*, trans. E.B. Ashton (London: Continuum, 1973) and Bruno Latour, *We Have Never Been Modern*, trans. Catherine Porter (Cambridge, MA: Harvard University Press, 1993).

134   See, among others, Jacques Derrida, *The Animal That Therefore I Am*, trans. Marie-Louis Mallet (New York: Fordham University Press, 2008) and Giorgio Agamben, *The Open: Man and Animal*, trans. Kevin Attell (Stanford: Stanford University Press, 2003).

permanently in tension with nature, but it was also a split that immediately divided the human being into two halves as both sovereign and subject.[135] How, then, is one to contemplate the theological distinction between the revealed and the natural in light of Manent's suggestion regarding sovereignty? The imposition of human sovereignty upon the divine is a basic, but recurring category mistake that needs to be re-examined not only so that the divine might be rethought, but so that the human (and the animal) might be reconceived as well.[136]

Dualistic thinking has permeated western thought since Plato, though it became firmly entrenched in metaphysical thinking through Aristotle's articulation of categorical oppositions (e.g. potentiality/actuality, necessity/contingency, and so forth).[137] One of the modern 'origins' of our dualisms can be found in the philosophy of René Descartes, who speculated that *cogito ergo sum* ('I think therefore I am'), and with this 'truth', a split between the mind and the body initiates a new intensity in our understanding of the human subject. This division of the subject is also traditionally seen in the work of Immanuel Kant on the *antinomies* of thought itself—those polarized oppositions that cannot be reconciled by the mind, and therefore serve as the two sides to every understanding. That is, we place our comprehension of a thing (concept, person, proposition) in-between two extremes in order to construct a representation in the first place. For him, the essential antinomies were: (1) the world has a beginning and is limited in space; the world has no beginning and is unlimited in space; (2) everything consists of simple parts; nothing is simple, all is complex; (3) all causality follows the laws of nature, hence determinism; everything is caused by the free properties of things, hence freedom; (4) there exists a necessary being, God; there is no necessary being, hence

---

135   Pierre Manent, *An Intellectual History of Liberalism*, trans. Rebecca Balinski (Princeton: Princeton University Press, 1995), pp. 114–117.

136   One of the largest problematics in theology—historically speaking—involves the contrast between a biblical (Hebrew) holistic view of the self and subsequent (Greek) dualistic Christian doctrines. How are we to understand their interaction? This begs one of the larger questions behind understanding the dualisms we construct, as such a 'whole' would perhaps deny the dualism. That is, is there any way to return to a holistic view beyond the dualisms (or dichotomies)? On the other hand, and as history then again teaches us, Christian doctrine and tradition are intertwined with Greek conceptual thought, and cannot simply be jettisoned.

137   In this context, it is insightful to read Adorno's commentary on Aristotle's *Metaphysics* in light of his eventual development of a negative dialectics. See Theodor W. Adorno, *Metaphysics: Concept and Problems*, ed. Rolf Tiedemann, trans. Edmund Jephcott (Stanford: Stanford University Press, 2001).

contingency, and possibly no God. Each proposition is fundamentally irreconcilable with its opposite, and this is what gives rise to thought in the first place, what allows reason and consciousness to exist.[138] They are central to western reasoning on the whole and their very existence perpetually begs the question: if Kant himself was unable to resolve these antinomies or dualisms of thought, and yet they continue to be problematic and the source of much political tension, is there anything we can do to them in order to break the impasse between their opposition?

My contention in the previous two parts is that we are at something of an impasse constituted by the continuous debate that rages between communitarian theologians, on the one hand, and continental philosophers, on the other, each of whom aim to present only one side of a dualistic and apparently irreplaceable tension between sovereign power and liberal discourse. The time has come, however, to pick up those threads of philosophical thought that seek to transcend this impasse, though not by making the same mistakes that Schmitt and Heidegger, among others, made—of attempting to uplift one side at the complete expense of the other. As some working in continental philosophical circles have already seen, there may be other ways to overcome the antinomies of representation as Kant had deduced them, allowing us to reformulate almost entirely the relationship between continental thought and theology. Indeed, the argument I am presenting here is that by looking at the ways we might otherwise deal with dualistic thought, we might actually pave a new road for the relationship between theology and continental philosophy to walk along together.

Rethinking the Role of Negativity in Continental Philosophy

As one possibility of dealing with dualistic thought, there is no doubt that a revisiting of negativity (and even nihilism) in continental thought is the most frequently taken up prospect for addressing the dualisms that undergird politics, religion, economics and philosophy in general. This was certainly what inspired Nietzsche to illuminate the dualism between Apollonian and Dionysian thinking, as well as his nihilistic efforts to go 'beyond good and evil'.[139] As

---

138 Immanuel Kant, *Critique of Pure Reason*, eds. and trans. Paul Guyer and Allen W. Wood (Cambridge: Cambridge University Press, 1997).

139 Friedrich Nietzsche, *The Birth of Tragedy*, trans. Walter Kaufmann (New York: Vintage, 1967) and *Beyond Good and Evil*, trans. R.J. Hollingdale (New York: Penguin, 1990). In a similar vein of genealogical pursuit, Adam Kotsko has recently sought to demonstrate how the figure of the devil is inseparable from western conceptualizations of an all-powerful God. See his *The Prince of This World* (Stanford: Stanford University Press, 2017).

Benjamin Noys has astutely pointed out, rehabilitating a concept of negativity has permeated continental thought in the 20th Century, permeating figures as diverse as Derrida, Deleuze, Latour, Negri and Badiou (his preferred subjects), but also, I would add, Adorno, Foucault, Agamben and Žižek.[140] Such an emphasis is likewise what spurred Ray Brassier's more recent *Nihil Unbound* to take up a radically negative path toward opening up the grounds for political and economic critique.[141] It is also what has given rise to an 'apology for nihilism' and 'weak thought' in general in the philosophy of Gianni Vattimo, as well as the 'nihilism of grace' in the more theologically focused writings of John Caputo.[142]

Nihilism is also, however, that which appears to most directly challenge the contents that theology attempts to preserve. In the words of Jean-Yves Lacoste, 'Theology is the guardian of all the meanings that nihilism abolishes [...]'.[143] Such a proposition would go some ways as well toward explaining why certain communitarians, especially those amongst the 'radically orthodox', have been so quick to label and dismiss those following specific genealogical-deconstructivist trains of continental philosophical work as exporting violent forms of nihilistic thought.[144]

In short, attempting to break these antinomic impasses has been the project of modern continental philosophy, as we see also in the work of Heidegger in other ways, and as was seen perhaps most explicitly in the work of Hegel before him. The Hegelian solution, which according to some is merely a synthesis of dualistic elements, has rather recently, according to others (i.e. Adorno, Žižek and Frederic Jameson, most notably), been taken as the negation of negation itself and not an implicitly positive or synthetic construct.[145] As the

---

140   Benjamin Noys, *The Persistence of the Negative: A Critique of Contemporary Continental Theory* (Edinburgh: Edinburgh University Press, 2010).

141   Ray Brassier, *Nihil Unbound: Enlightenment and Extinction* (Basingstoke: Palgrave Macmillan, 2007).

142   Gianni Vattimo, *The End of Modernity: Nihilism and Hermeneutics in Postmodern Culture*, trans. Jon R. Snyder (Baltimore, MD: Johns Hopkins University Press, 1988) and John D. Caputo, *The Insistence of God: A Theology of Perhaps* (Bloomington, IN: Indiana University Press, 2013), as well as *The Weakness of God: A Theology of the Event* (Bloomington, IN: Indiana University Press, 2006).

143   Jean-Yves Lacoste, *From Theology to Theological Thinking*, trans. W. Chris Hackett (Charlottesville, VA: University of Virginia Press, 2014), p. 86.

144   Perhaps the best example would be the repeated invectives of John Milbank. See also Conor Cunningham, *Genealogy of Nihilism* (London: Routledge, 2002).

145   Žižek, *Less Than Nothing* and Frederic Jameson, *Valences of the Dialectic* (London: Verso, 2009). It is Žižek's practical negative dialectics, I would argue, that aligns his work most

foundation for what we might follow Adorno in calling a 'negative dialectics', the negation of negation itself goes beyond dualistic thinking insofar as it places its emphasis not on favoring one side over another (*the* political theological mistake Schmitt and others have succumbed to), nor in achieving some synthetic and wholly artificial 3rd term, but in further negating one reductionistic (read: already negated) side in the dualism.[146] This is what Jean Wahl had once called the 'negativity of negativity' that leads implicitly to the 'transcendence of transcendence' or a form of 'trans-immanence', as Jean-Luc Nancy has put it.[147] We are offered, through such a negative dialectics, with even the deconstruction of deconstructionism that potentially opens a pathway toward non-dualistic thought.[148]

The issue of violence arises here too as an essential structural feature of the formation of representations themselves. Every representation is, more or less, a reduction of the 'thing itself'—a putting of a 'natural' thing into a 'box' (or category, or concept) so that we can understand it and talk about it (make a definition of it, make words, have language, etc.). For example, perhaps the friend/enemy distinction (definitions essential to our political dwelling) can be undone by realizing that we are enemies to ourselves even, and that identifying the enemy is often harder than we think.[149] This is what the realization

---

    directly with those other 'counter traditions' that oppose a sovereign, metaphysical deity. Such a reading runs parallel to that made by Adam Kotsko in his *Žižek and Theology* (London: T&T Clark, 2008). It is in this sense that one should pay attention to Žižek's development of a 'negative materialist theology'. See, among other places in his work, Slavoj Žižek, *Disparities* (London: Bloomsbury, 2016). I would place alongside these readings of Hegel that of Catherine Malabou as well. See her *The Future of Hegel: Plasticity, Temporality and Dialectic*, trans. Lisabeth During (London: Routledge, 2005).

146 See, among other places in his work, Theodor W. Adorno, *An Introduction to Dialectics*, ed. Christoph Ziermann (Cambridge: Polity, 2017).

147 See, among other places, Jean-Luc Nancy, *The Inoperative Community*, ed. Peter Connor, trans. Peter Connor et al. (Minneapolis, MN: University of Minnesota Press, 1991) and Jean Wahl, *Human Existence and Transcendence*, ed. and trans. William C. Hackett (Notre Dame, IN: University of Notre Dame Press, 2016), pp. 26–28. I would also draw attention to how such projects share in Adorno's negative dialectical thought in the formation of what Patrice Haynes has called an 'immanent transcendence'. See her *Immanent Transcendence: Reconfiguring Materialism in Continental Philosophy* (London: Bloomsbury, 2012).

148 David Loy, *Nonduality: A Study in Comparative Philosophy* (New York: Humanity, 1988), p. 293.

149 Gil Anidjar's *The Jew, The Arab*, deals with the problematics of defining the enemy (against whom a Just War may presumably be fought) in Aquinas and Augustine. They are both clear that the enemy should be defeated, on moral grounds, but determining the enemy is actually the larger problem. Are we so sure we can identify who an enemy really is? Is the

of a negative dialectics looks like in more fully conceived concrete terms for established identities and communities.

Though some have argued that it is Christianity itself that must be overcome in order to inspire a non-dualistic (non-Christian) 'pagan' theology, there are resources within Christianity itself that speak to how dualistic thinking might be overcome.[150] Indeed, there is something like a negative dialectic active within the heart of Christian mystical traditions that offers us the negation of negation itself and so of the dualism that would permanently contrast the positive (*kataphatic*) with the negative (*apophatic*).[151] There may also be a possible solution to such rigid dichotomies—and here following Agamben's reading of Pauline letters—by 'dividing division' itself, as he claims Saint Paul once did in attempting to go beyond the male/female, slave/free, Jew/Greek divisions that characterized his society.[152] This may be the only way to retain *difference* and yet to remove the force of the boundaries themselves, not doing away with them, but undoing their normative force when such force is unjust. In many ways, this is to recall Jesus' claim that he did not come to do away with the law (of representations, hence of these dichotomies of understanding, as much as of the Torah and its laws), but to *fulfill* it. It is nothing less than *this* fulfillment that we in fact need to understand in greater depth in order to facilitate a rethinking of the dualistic logics that continue to divide humanity into numerous categories.

Despite demonstrating how these facile dualities often reinforce existing violent and political paradigms, political power continues to rely upon such dualistic frameworks in order to assert a polarized matrix of representation, though there are signs too of its weakening in a contemporary context. The traditional dualisms that have structured theological and philosophical thought for centuries have been challenged by non-dualistic ways of thinking, often probing the depths of comparative analysis in general.[153] The rise and popularity

---

one we are so opposed to so absolutely unlike us? And are those so close to us fundamentally our friends? What is the truly porous nature of the boundaries between friend and enemy, in our personal, social and also national contexts?

150   See Anthony T. Kronman, *Confessions of a Born-Again Pagan* (New Haven, CT: Yale University Press, 2016), pp. 1022–1023.
151   See the discussion of the second negation that qualifies Christian mystical theologies in Denys Turner, *The Darkness of God: Negativity in Christian Mysticism* (Cambridge: Cambridge University Press, 1995) and Deirdre Carabine, *The Unknown God: Negative Theology in the Platonic Tradition: Plato to Eriugena* (Eugene, OR: Wipf & Stock, 1995).
152   Agamben, *The Time that Remains*.
153   Michelle Voss Roberts, *Dualities: A Theology of Difference* (Louisville, KY: Westminster John Knox Press, 2010).

of political and contextual (liberation, feminist, black, latino/a, queer and so forth) theologies have also testified to a decline of systematic thought, highlighting the myriad violences of social, political and economic oppression while simultaneously pointing toward non-western ways of performing theological investigations. The fragmentation of theology in the late modern period is not coincidental then to the rise of political theology, but rather generated by a form of non-dualistic negative dialectics that have challenged established dialectical theologies by privileging non-identity over identity, and giving rise explicitly as well to Jürgen Moltmann's ostensibly political theology (which he claimed descended directly from Adorno's negative dialectics), the forerunner to contemporary contextual and liberation theologies.[154] The dissemination of negative dialectics within the various fields of contextual theology has thereby shifted the theologian's gaze to other oppressed or marginalized groups, often in global contexts that defy the underlying duality that has traditionally governed theological thought: the division between the West and the non-West.[155]

We might note too in this context how Bruno Latour's intuition that religious modes of existence are fundamentally different than political ones is an analysis that contains the unexplored possibility of rereading political-theological relations beyond the dualities that have generally confined them, opening such a discourse toward a greater degree of complexity.[156] Such research into these various modes of existence, taken alongside his specific critique of modernity, would allow us to rethink theological discourse from the ground up in a modern context. Such a 'speculative grace' (in opposition to the transcendent grace/immanent nature dualism), as Adam Miller has helpfully defined it in the context of Latour's work specifically, displaces the traditional dualities we have come to rely on in western thought, and to learn, perhaps for the first time on a global scale, what a genuine act of hospitality might mean for theological and philosophical discourse.[157] By putting Latour's work in dialogue with the contemporary fields of complexity and actor-network theory, I believe we might be able to provide a renewed perspective for theology that

---

154 Bruce L. McCormack, *Karl Barth's Critically Realistic Dialectical Theology: Its Genesis and Development, 1909–1936* (Oxford: Clarendon Press, 1997), as well as Moltmann, *The Crucified God*.

155 Edward Said, *Culture and Imperialism* (New York: Vintage, 1994).

156 Bruno Latour, *Rejoicing: Or the Torments of Religious Speech*, trans. Julie Rose (Cambridge: Polity, 2013), Latour, *An Inquiry into Modes of Existence*, and Gilbert Simondon, *On the Mode of Existence of Technical Objects*, trans. Cecile Malaspina (Minneapolis, MN: Univocal, 2016).

157 Adam S. Miller, *Speculative Grace: Bruno Latour and Object-Oriented Theology* (New York: Fordham University Press, 2013).

has deep resonances with ways in which the field has recently been drifting over the course of modernity.[158] In this too, I believe, we could find another resonance which such notions of complexity hold with modern and contemporary theories on the complex probabilities that bring a person to faith, such as we find in John Henry Newman's work, as well as within comparative theological methods that are currently challenging our most essential theological foundations.[159]

As but merely a suggestion in the direction of a critical, nondualistic theology, and through sources that are rarely brought together, we might find great benefit in addressing the 'cross-pressures' that can be said to establish religious identity within our modern secular age precipitating a reflection on the use of language, thereby also making Charles Taylor's work central to the present inquiry.[160] If indeed language shapes human experience in its multiple dimensions, then ascertaining the role that dualisms play in establishing the political-theological coordinates of our existence is a necessary inquiry. Refusing to reduce the complexity of such cross-pressures in the formation of religious and secular identities, then, would only enhance our present descriptive capabilities. To assist in this understanding, we might too bring in the voice of Jean-François Lyotard, whose discussion of the 'differend', or the impasse that results when we are unable to reach an aesthetic or political judgment would be most helpful in complimenting Taylor's efforts to locate the failures of modern subjectivity.[161] Something like the addition of Lyotard's insights might also provide us with a philosophical tool through which to assess Taylor's work on language and the seemingly irreconcilable differences that

---

158 David Byrne and Gillian Callaghan, *Complexity Theory and the Social Sciences: The State of the Art* (London: Routledge; Meadows, 2013), Donella H. Meadows, *Thinking in Systems: A Primer*, ed. Diana Wright, (White River Junction, VT: Chelsea Green, 2008) and M. Mitchell Waldrop, *Complexity: The Emerging Science at the Edge of Order and Chaos* (New York: Simon and Schuster, 1992).

159 John Henry Newman, *Fifteen Sermons Preached Before the University of Oxford Between A.D. 1826 and 1843* (Notre Dame, IN: University of Notre Dame Press, 1997) as well as his *An Essay in Aid of a Grammar of Assent* (Cambridge: Cambridge University Press, 2010). See also Joseph Stephen O'Leary, *Conventional and Ultimate Truth: A Key for Fundamental Theology* (Notre Dame, IN: University of Notre Dame Press, 2015).

160 Charles Taylor, *A Secular Age*, Cambridge, MA: Belknap, 2007), as well as his more recent *The Language Animal: The Full Shape of the Human Linguistic Capacity* (Cambridge, MA: Belknap, 2016).

161 Lyotard, *The Differend*. See also Lieven Boeve, *Lyotard and Theology* (London: T&T Clark, 2014).

arise within the modern, hybrid cross-pressures that fail to fully identify those dwelling in a Western context.

One of the main problems we encounter in this narrative of things, however, is that our cultural inquiry is bound to another, often unnoticed and inherently dualistic framework, not only in terms of our preferred linguistic representations (western languages or non-western languages), but especially in terms of this dualistic division between the West and every other point of view not in dialogue with the West (traditionally the 'East', but really anything not-western would suffice). Breaking down this dualism which lies beneath our most essential historical, political, cultural, economic and religious representations is necessary for an authentically comparative philosophy that deepens the complexity of relations rather than re-inscribe them into a binary dualism.[162] Indeed, critiques of binary (dualistic) systems have been most prevalent recently in feminist and queer theories, though theology is still needing to understand and assess this limitation more than it has within the subfields of contextual theology alone.[163] Rather theologians, and philosophers too for that matter, must attend to the ways in which a nondualistic, non-binary way of thinking moves us closer to complex and comparative studies beyond what we have previously known. Indeed, there are a limited number of only recently appearing studies devoted to exploring the possibility of existence for fields of comparative theology and philosophy alike.[164]

It should be duly noted, however, that this general trajectory of thinking beyond dualisms and the field of representations is precisely what has defined continental philosophical thinking over the past century or so. This failure of dualistic identities—a point that surfaces, again, on the heels of an analysis of (non)identity resulting from a negative dialectics—can also be located, theologically-speaking, in recent developments of comparative theology and interreligious dialogue, whose methods underline the need to rethink theological foundations in our world.[165] Research along these lines would also, and

---

162 The facile East/West division that underlies global political interaction is critiqued with force in the work of Edward Said, among others.

163 Julie L. Nagoshi and Craig T. Nagoshi, *Gender and Sexual Identity: Transcending Feminist and Queer Theory* (New York: Springer, 2014).

164 See, among others, Tim Connolly, *Doing Philosophy Comparatively* (London: Bloomsbury, 2015).

165 Francis X. Clooney, *Comparative Theology: Deep Learning Across Religious Borders*, Oxford: Wiley-Blackwell, 2010), Hugh Nicholson, *Comparative Theology and the Problem of Religious Rivalry* (Oxford: Oxford University Press, 2011), and Marianne Moyaert, *In Response to the Religious Other: Ricoeur and the Fragility of Interreligious Encounters* (Lexington, KY: Lexington Books, 2014).

as I intend to demonstrate in the sections that follow, point in the direction of a comparative analysis of the present research with recent efforts to find a way beyond dualistic thinking through a variety of approaches that I will conclude this all-too-brief study with as signs of future exploration in relations between theology and continental philosophy.[166] In order, I will provide three short vignettes on (1) the works of William Desmond and Diana Eck in dialogue with one another, (2) a particular position staked out by Joeri Schrijvers and (3) a general exposition of a phenomenological 'solution' to many of the problematics I have sketched so far.

William Desmond and Diana Eck on Porousness

The Irish-born continental philosopher William Desmond's formulation of 'being between', what he terms the 'metaxological way', is an idea that, I believe, allows us to further deepen challenges to specific cultural binary divisions, while also establishing a position from which to develop political positions beyond established ones, whatever this might mean in the reality of our limited linguistic representations. For his part, Desmond is concerned with trying to think systematically 'beyond the system', a project which, philosophically, allows him to push the boundaries of thought while also being mindful that, despite our ability to 'overdetermine' our being, as he puts it, we will nevertheless return to the typical categorizations that characterize both thought and language.[167] He is interested in promoting a religious poetics that exceeds determination, but also that allows for determination to be yet possible. He seeks, to be more precise, what he labels a 'porous' system that allows for various flows to meander their way through what appears to us as even the most impermeable of systems. In political-theological terms, this means being open to a form of 'communal agapeic service' that is beyond both sovereignty and servility, as he puts it.[168]

The intricacies of Desmond's philosophy are unveiled most directly in his elaboration of the fourfold sense of being, or the four ways by which we approach determination. First among these is the *univocal* sense, one that seeks to determine definition through an imposition of sameness and the removal of difference. There is no doubt that such a sense provides us with a good many

---

166 In this conclusion, I somewhat follow the lead taken already in Emmanuel Falque, *Crossing the Rubicon: The Borderlands of Philosophy and Theology*, trans. Reuben Shank and Matthew Farley (New York: Fordham University Press, 2016).
167 William Desmond, *God and the Between* (Oxford: Wiley-Blackwell, 2008), p. 10.
168 William Desmond, *The Intimate Universal: The Hidden Porosity Among Religion, Art, Philosophy, and Politics* (New York: Columbia University Press, 2016), p. 179.

of the platforms by which we stage the various levels of intelligibility, but it likewise denies us, at times, the flexibility that accurately characterizes humanity. The second sense, therefore, is the *equivocal*, or that which revels in difference and acknowledges the perplexity of our existence. Its descent into the multiplicity of difference is a helpful corrective to the first sense, perhaps, but it can also lead to the loss of meaning. Though the first two senses are often taken as a dualistic impasse (and this is how I have been discussing them in the above tensions between communitarians and genealogical-deconstructivists), the third sense, and one that deceptively appears to resolve the problems that arise in the first two senses, is that of a *dialectics* which offers a more 'subtle' sense of oneness in that it accounts for differences as it tries to 'finesse' its way beyond them. It is an inclusive sense of sameness, then, to be sure, but one that nonetheless reduces difference to sameness in order to achieve synthesis (e.g. as most, but not all, have read Hegel's dialectics). The fourth sense, and the one that Desmond ultimately champions, is the *metaxological* way or that which points toward a 'pluralized intermediation' of being.[169] The metaxological is, for Desmond, a way of 'being between' things, a suspended dialectics, if you will, that refuses '[...] the claim to have categories to determine finally what itself outstrips every categorical determination'.[170] From this vantage point, philosophy, in its ever-present desires to deliver us categorical, systematic certainty must become open to something like a religious poetics that moves beyond every determination, just as any identity—or equally every dissolution of identity—must learn to locate itself between every determination that is made.

If Desmond's considerations sound a bit like the various theorists of exile that litter the field of poetry or of negative dialectics, this is not a coincidence, for his understanding of our identity finds a solid echo with such reflections. It is the case, in fact, that a metaxological sense of our being throws us out beyond where we had thought ourselves to be located—Desmond's word for this act is 'hyperbole', or that which throws us above our determinations[171]—and it is only through such a 'throwing' beyond and above that we have the chance to engage the true 'goodness' of our being in relation to others, always between others, the 'agapeics of communication', as he puts it.[172] Such a way of being is importantly not limited to those 'on the margins' or those 'in the middle', but

---

169 Desmond, *God and the Between*, p. 117.
170 Desmond, *God and the Between*, p. 117.
171 Desmond, *God and the Between*, pp. 126–128.
172 Desmond, *God and the Between*, p. 150.

pushes us outward from wherever we are to wherever the other already is.[173] In this sense, and here is where I locate his originality in suggesting this, we are challenged to go beyond even Deleuze and Guattari's 'minor' groupings and to find the principle of exile that lies at the heart of all discourses and identities.[174] There is yet a chance to be engaged with the other no matter what our starting point for engaging them might be, as if (crucially) either side in a dualistic impasse might be divided from within. The poverty of the self, for Desmond, is certainly the 'stripping of false selves', and a faint echo of Deleuze and Guattari's act of de-territorialization.[175] It is also an opening, or unblocking of flows, a *porosity*, that leads us toward '[...] something that is not any one thing, something more an energy, an energy that seems like nothing, that passes or is communicated from one to another'.[176]

In Desmond's understanding 'the system' which forms our 'systematics' is always exposed to the potential for totalizing its claims and in the process closing itself off to that exterior, primordial openness which should characterize our being. Religious poetics, then, comes to stand for an original porosity of being which is 'mindful attentiveness to coming to be'.[177] As that which 'exceeds the system', religious poetics encompasses an original sense of being which is 'prior to being artistic and being philosophical': 'There is an original sense of being religious which is granted in the poetics of the given porosity of our being'.[178] Being open to the transcendence of God means then a recognition from both ends of the spectrum (systematic thought and religious poetics) of a mutual need for interaction. Desmond therefore points toward something like a 'poetics of the divine' which precedes any attempt to univocalize being.[179] Returning to this theme at the end of his work *God and the Between*, Desmond has leave to remark that 'created poetry has all the moving power of utterance

---

173   Desmond, *God and the Between*, p. 164.
174   In a certain sense, however, it could no doubt be argued that Deleuze and Guattari's 'minor' literature at the heart of all 'major' literatures is really operative on the same plane as Desmond's 'being between', though it takes the standpoint of the 'minor' perspective. See Gilles Deleuze and Félix Guattari, *Kafka: Toward a Minor Literature*, trans. Dana Polan (Minneapolis, MN: University of Minnesota Press, 1986).
175   William Desmond, *Is There a Sabbath for Thought? Between Religion and Philosophy* (New York: Fordham University Press, 2005), p. 22. See also Gilles Deleuze and Félix Guattari, *A Thousand Plateaus: Capitalism and Schizophrenia*, trans. Brian Massumi (Minneapolis, MN: University of Minnesota Press, 1987).
176   Desmond, *Is There a Sabbath for Thought?*, p. 24.
177   Desmond, *God and the Between*, p. 10.
178   Desmond, *God and the Between*, p. 11.
179   Desmond, *God and the Between*, p. 73.

and the saturated density of mystery we find in great art. We need something of divine finesse to hear or see or decipher this art'.[180] As he continues,

> Creation is divine poetics but it is not for the good of God's own self-poiesis that the world is. Because God is agapeically poetic, the world as art is for the sake of its own good. And what is its own good? That, being good, it realizes the promise of agapeic being. This means that it be like God. This is most fully manifested in the between in the community of agapeic service.[181]

Providing us with a comprehensive model by which to digest the various approaches one might take with regard to global, religious diversity, contemporary theologian Diana Eck unfolds three possible scenarios of religious belief and interaction, which I want to discuss in light of Desmond's typology of the four senses of being. Though the framework of interreligious dialogue might appear to some to be at quite a remove from continental philosophy, I want to argue that they are not so distant as we might at first glance suspect—especially, as already noted, as both rely upon and try to answer the existence of dualistic frameworks of understanding. Hence, they converge in a very specific way that I want to unfold more fully so that we might be able to view the aims of continental philosophy anew.

For Eck, the three responses generally given to the pluralism inherent in our world today are the *exclusivist* position (i.e. there is only one view of the divine and our religion possess it), the *inclusivist* position (i.e. our religion possesses the truth, but other faiths have partial views that can be included within our own) and the *pluralist* position (every religion has a limited view on the divine, as it transcends any single religious viewpoint, which is ultimately a negative theological perspective).[182] As one might easily conceive, these models mirror Desmond's fourfold scheme almost entirely, though the equivocal sense has dropped out of Eck's models, mainly, I would wager, because it does not yield itself to any coherent representational position that one might take (though it is a helpful and necessary deconstructive tool at the heart of continental philosophy, as I have already sought to demonstrate). With this exception accounted for, it becomes easier to discern how the *exclusivist* maintains a *univocal* sense of identity, the *inclusivist* operates a *dialectical* method for

---

180 Desmond, *God and the Between*, p. 323.
181 Desmond, *God and the Between*, pp. 329–330.
182 Diana L. Eck, *Encountering God: A Spiritual Journey from Bozeman to Banaras* (Boston: Beacon, 1993), p. 50.

assimilating the other's point of view and the *pluralist* searches for a way of 'being between' the various positions (hence, its *metaxological* nature) without assimilating the other into its own way of being. By explicating these three productive categories, Eck, for her part, is able to demonstrate the practical (and political) viability of Desmond's philosophy within a theological context, showing us its potential strengths and weaknesses alike. In this sense, the theological constitutes a field of praxis upon which the theoretical structures are tested and proven.

What Eck will conclude when faced with these three options, and in such a way as to challenge Desmond's perhaps somewhat abstract and idealized choice for a permanent position of 'being between', is that, in order to be intellectually honest, we should strive for the pluralist (metaxological) position of 'being between' different religious traditions, but that we also may have to settle for the inclusivist (dialectical) viewpoint insofar as it is the bedrock language with which we comprehend and discuss our world.[183] In her estimation, we *need* labels and representations, as inaccurate as they will be, in order to make sense of our world and communicate something about it to others. The inevitability of this compromised position is a reflection of the linguistic and cultural reality in which we dwell. As she puts it, 'As long as we hold the religious insights of our particular traditions, cast in our particular languages, to be in some sense universal, we cannot avoid speaking at times in an inclusivist way. It is important to recognize this'.[184] What is yet 'unsettling' in this solution to the problem, however, is that, according to Eck, we are entirely bound to only one language '[...] to make definitive claims about the whole of reality', which is presumably much larger than any single language.[185] There is an obvious contradiction, or paradox, in holding this position, but it is one that we simply cannot do without—and despite the fact that we prefer our religious claims to appear as 'absolute', something they may never be able to achieve as we might otherwise prefer.

What Eck calls to our attention, and this is what unites the many disparate threads within the present inquiry, is *the* inherent problem of language itself, but also of religion and of politics too: we desire to access the 'thing itself', the object 'in itself' that lies behind the words but which is also forever just out of our reach, no matter if this is some remote and distant object or thing, another person standing before us or an emotion, taste, scent or the like. We seek a purer access to such *things*, but we always fall short and we will continue to

---

183   Eck, *Encountering God*, p. 170.
184   Eck, *Encountering God*, p. 180.
185   Eck, *Encountering God*, p. 184.

do so forever. Part of being human, we must admit again and again, is that we construct representations of such things, but we cannot actually broach the sanctity of their 'true' nature. But press on we must, and we do. The normative construction is cast aside, but another one is immediately made. In a certain sense, such representations can become yet another golden calf we falsely worship, or they can emerge as a divine injunction pointing beyond the reality we see before our eyes. In this, we might say, we are not to smooth over the cracks and fissures, but, following Ellen Armour, to deepen them and expose them even further.[186] In so many words, the only accurate representation we can give is one that exposes its own failure to represent the 'thing itself'.[187]

I am reminded at this point of Derrida's presentation of an antinomy of language that perpetually shapes us: we only ever speak one language; we never speak only one language.[188] This is a tension that we are continuously bound up within and which we cannot escape. But it is also the signal of the limitation of our linguistic and religious selves. No representation, theological or otherwise, will be able to capture the 'thing itself', especially the complex and multifaceted person who stands before us in their dazzling wonder.

Joeri Schrijvers on a Ground between Faith and Belief

The apparent impasse between phenomenology and deconstruction that Joeri Schrijvers seeks to overcome through a reasoned analysis of the underlying issue between these paths of inquiry is one that, to my mind, opens up a political conversation on just how such impasses—often conceived in overly simplified and frequently polarized dualistic terms—allow us to reread the field and operations of theology and continental philosophy on the whole.[189] What such a philosophical impasse parallels, I would argue, is nothing short of the basic coordinates for the field of political theology, much as Schmitt had once sought to define it: sovereignty, on the one hand, and democratic-liberalism, on the other, locked in fierce opposition to one another and with neither seemingly willing to relinquish control for a moment to the other. For Schmitt, the apparent failures of democratic-liberalism meant that some form of monarchal (even perhaps papal) sovereignty needed to be reasserted in the modern

---

186   Ellen T. Armour, *Deconstruction, Feminist Theology, and the Problem of Difference: Subverting the Race/Gender Divide* (Chicago: University of Chicago Press, 1999), p. 182.
187   See the articulation and illustration of this point as given in Judith Butler, *Frames of War: When Is Life Grievable?* (London: Verso, 2010).
188   Jacques Derrida, *Monolinguism of the Other: Or, The Prosthesis of Origin*, trans. Patrick Mensah (Stanford: Stanford University Press, 1998).
189   See, among other places in his work, Schrijvers, *Ontotheological Turnings?*

era against the nation-state's indebtedness to far weaker political forms, as I have already noted. The strength of the sovereign was the only thing that could guarantee the continuance of the state in the face of its enemies. Though Schmitt's choice for dictatorship (and consequently Nazism) was tragically flawed, his general analysis of the political field and its theological roots yields significant insight into how the fields of politics and theology alike are themselves structured.

Overlaying Schmitt's formulations upon Schrijvers' analysis, we can perhaps begin to see the same impasse located within theology wherein the anti-metaphysical side ('liberal-democratic') engages in an 'endless conversation' and espouses a tendency toward absolute secularization, while refusing to concede that there may yet be a need for onto-theology ('sovereignty') in the end—something that theological communitarians either overtly or inadvertently support. I believe this overlay is justified, not only by the range of figures that Schrijvers has chosen to study (i.e. John Caputo, Jean-Luc Nancy, Peter Sloterdijk, Jacques Derrida and Jean-Luc Marion, among others), but also because he concludes his work with an explicit call to avoid authoritative (authoritarian) and sovereign movements alongside the ever-present quests within continental philosophy to avoid the metaphysics that legitimates such positions.[190] Espousing such a position is not easy to do, however, and this is what elevates Schrijver's work above so much else that is out there already.

A major claim of his argument is that one cannot wholly abstract themselves into the 'endless conversation' that refuses to make a decision and arrive at an ontic form of existence. There must be some way to articulate the necessity of sovereignty without it becoming the 'dictatorship' of tradition, as Schrijvers phrases things.[191] Keeping in mind the parallels I am suggesting, Schmitt's failure had been to attempt a defense of monarchical sovereignty as a form of dictatorship. What Schrijvers illuminates is rather how, in the face of those who would simply strive to dismantle metaphysics entirely (and here his critique of Caputo's criticisms of sovereignty are particularly interesting to follow), there is yet another possibility routinely overlooked by both sides: (abstract) faith needs (embodied) belief in order to be phenomenologically possible in this world. The problem, as he stakes it, is that the world has been severed from love and love from world by these, or similar, negative political theologies bent on the act of deconstructing only.[192] If it is possible to have

---

190 Joeri Schrijvers, *Between Faith and Belief: Toward a Contemporary Phenomenology of Religious Life* (Albany, NY: State University of New York Press, 2016), pp. 297–302.
191 Schrijvers, *Between Faith and Belief*, p. 292.
192 Schrijvers, *Between Faith and Belief*, p. 300.

something like a 'faith without faith' in purely structural and abstract, even intellectual terms (much as Derrida or Caputo had put it), belief is the embodied side of life, what makes love a reality and a transformative one at that. Though Caputo himself has often seen a similar need to merge the concrete, historical with the abstract philosophical or theological (see his *On Religion*, for example[193]), Schrijvers wants to deepen the relationship between faith and belief to more than an unexplainable reality; he wants to make a philosophical argument for why these two must co-exist.

Relying on the writings of Ludwig Binswanger, Schijvers develops an incarnational theology of love as a form of intersubjectivity that takes our ontic reality, our traditions, institutions and religions more seriously than the negative political theologians might typically concede. Binswanger's openness to a form of existence between sovereignty and liberalism gives us another way to contemplate the political impasse that dwells at the heart of theological debate and exposes another avenue for the future of political theology in general. There will not be a 'post-metaphysical' era envisioned as 'post-Christian' in a western context because we are not able to extricate ourselves from the ostensibly Christian onto-theological foundations that undergird every attempt to form a 'religion without religion' or a deconstruction of Christianity. The anarchy, Gnosticism, antinomianism and apocalypticism of the negative political theologians such as Nancy, Derrida, Caputo and Sloterdijk (but one could also add Agamben, Crockett, Robbins and a host of others, as I have already mentioned) have a significant role to play in terms of deconstructing the onto-theological foundations of metaphysics in order to expose their potentially violent substructure. But it is also a substructure we cannot simply remove from existence altogether.

Schrijvers, for his part, is focused on a philosophy of incarnation that takes our material existence seriously and confirms how meaning does arise from matter, as he puts is.[194] There is in the mix a certain paradox of existence that refuses to yield absolute certainty—what makes us ultimately 'beings in default'—and this is the very condition of what being immersed in both faith and belief is about: 'Coming to terms with such a being in default may be the adequate response to the end of metaphysics: it is to recognize that we all share in this default and this lack and that this "knowing of not knowing" is what turns philosophy, as the love of wisdom, into a wisdom of love: not to overcome the lack, but to love even the lack (of rationality, of ultimate meaning)'.[195]

---

193 John D. Caputo, *On Religion* (London: Routlege, 2001).
194 Schrijvers, *Between Faith and Belief*, p. 304.
195 Schrijvers, *Between Faith and Belief*, pp. 304–305.

Trying to permanently overcome such a lack is the temptation of sovereignty, one that has certainly brought a fair share of totalitarian forms into our world. Failing to grasp that we need some form of metaphysics, and its accompanying sense of sovereignty, in material form is the temptation of the negative political theologians, one that exposes them to frequent charges of nihilism. Both extremes are to be avoided, of course, as the 'being in default' that we are is an inescapable being in poverty (cf. Agamben's work on an ontology of poverty, or Emmanuel Falque and Jean-Yves Lacoste on poverty in phenomenological terms).[196]

What results for Schrijvers is a theological agnosticism wherein one does not know if one is included (politically, theologically) in whatever community that surrounds them but knows only that they must not be involved in a 'politics of being' that entails exclusion. The 'politics of being' that he calls for is one that involves 'the minute, meticulous and phenomenological assessment of the concrete differences between particular traditions, be they religious (Caputo) or ontological (Nancy)'.[197] In this politics, something like an intricate and complex network of relations becomes slightly more visible and just possibly more comprehensible (as in the work of Latour, I might suggest, which pursues the intricate networks of meaning bound up in the various 'modes of existence' in our world). Such a politics of being, which perhaps shares a good deal with existentialism in some respects, might also open the door toward greater interreligious and comparative theological understandings. It might also, if we can see nearly as far as Schrijvers projects, bring a renewed appreciation of secular, agnostic *and* pagan traditions vis-à-vis traditional theological ones. This possibility is what allows something like Nancy's or Lacoste's focus on the 'pagan residue in Christianity' to exist and take on renewed significance in that such a move dictates a reality wherein 'each and every person who attempts to be Christian is first and foremost insufficiently Christian'.[198] Every identity is ultimately undone at the same moment that the person who held that identity realizes how they are so much more than whatever had previously claimed them. What I see unfolding in his work is a most insightful account of how we might address the historical field of theological (and political) operations anew, refusing the polarized dichotomies that often lump people into overly facile conservative and liberal, sovereign and democratic, counterparts.

---

196   See Giorgio Agamben, *The Highest Poverty: Monastic Rules and Form-of-Life*, trans. Adam Kotsko (Stanford: Stanford University Press, 2013) and Lacoste, *Experience and the Absolute*.
197   Schrijvers, *Between Faith and Belief*, p. 300.
198   Schrijvers, *Between Faith and Belief*, p. 315.

A Phenomenological Way Forward

> Today philosophy seems to have forgotten *the honor of the theological.*
> EMMANUEL FALQUE[199]

In large measure, what Desmond and Schrijvers present us with is an argument that runs parallel to much of what contemporary continental philosophy finds most suggestive in the form of a 'postmodern apologetics', as Christina Gschwandtner has labeled it, or that which focuses on the excesses that go beyond any normative boundary and which certainly inform a good deal of theological speculation on the nature of transcendence.[200] There is no doubt that such transgressive or ek-static conditions vis-à-vis normativity, identity, materiality and logic in general are what has motivated much of contemporary continental thought, from Heidegger to Derrida and from Foucault to Agamben.[201] This focus on excess has similarly crept into and buoyed the works of George Bataille, Maurice Blanchot, Jacques Lacan and Gilles Deleuze, to indicate but a handful of more prominent names.

What we are concerned with now is in large measure locating, as Emmanuel Falque has put it, those '*philosophema* that are at the same time *theologoumena*', which he finds illuminated directly in phenomenological focal points 'such as Levinas's face, Chrétien's speech, Henry's flesh, Marion's gift, Lacoste's liturgy'.[202] Following Edmund Husserl's initial investigations into such territory to access the 'things themselves', but clearly going beyond him as well, these material moments of potential transcendence present within the phenomenological analysis of one's ek-static existence indicate not just the possibility of the theological within what had appeared as merely philosophical, but also how we might be able, at long last, to 'cross the rubicon', as Falque has imagined, in order to conceive of how hermeneutics, phenomenology, deconstruction and genealogy all share in a common focus that has often not been seen. In other words, the methods and aims of phenomenology are not as removed from those of the genealogist-archaeologists as one might at first suspect—and as I spoke of earlier as a possible 'fracture' within continental

---

199   Falque, *Crossing the Rubicon*, p. 129.
200   Gschwandtner, *Postmodern Apologetics?*
201   It is particularly noteworthy to see how the desire to exceed normative boundaries made an impact on the personal and professional lives of these philosophers. See, for example, James Miller, *The Passion of Michel Foucault* (New York: Simon & Schuster, 1993).
202   Falque, *Crossing the Rubicon*, p. 158.

thought—especially as both fields are intimately acquainted with the desire for the origins of knowledge.[203]

Moreover, these subfields of continental thought are not far removed from critical theory's understanding of itself, much as Adorno once pointed out in his admittance that there was a profound similarity between negative dialectics and the phenomenological reduction that could yield very interesting results if pursued further.[204] In this light, Jean-Luc Marion's reading of the mystical traditions in order to confirm the double negation, or negation of negation, as *the* fundamental movement of both mystical theology and the phenomenological reduction would only seem to further cement this union of interests in some manner.[205] Bound up with those negative theologies that recognize the need for a second negation (a negation of negation itself then, or of whatever has been imposed upon a more fluid and excessive existence, as with a name such as 'God') and not simply a negation of whatever positive content has been derived is part and parcel of the phenomenological reduction and, as such, deserves to be reconsidered in light of critical-theoretical writings on phenomenological method.[206]

What this double negation implies, and as we have seen already in Desmond and Schrijvers, is that particular material realities are not able to contain the excessive qualities that inhabit them, which allows Marion in this case to formulate his most popularized conceptualization, that of the saturated phenomena. Saturated phenomena, as he describes them, give humanity access to an excessiveness that is made available through the materiality of existence.[207] In the presence of such an almost sacramental experience, humanity is able to perceive something that actually goes beyond existence but which existence somehow also records the trace of.

---

203   See the argument made in Rodolphe Gasché, 'Something Like an Archaeology', *The Honor of Thinking: Critique, Theory, Philosophy* (Stanford: Stanford University Press, 2007), pp. 211–249.

204   Theodor W. Adorno, *Lectures on Negative Dialectics: Fragments of a Lecture Course 1965/1966*, ed. Rolf Tiedemann, trans. Rodney Livingstone (Cambridge: Polity, 2008), p. 118.

205   Thomas A. Carlson, *Indiscretion: Finitude and the Naming of God* (Chicago: University of Chicago Press, 1999).

206   Jean-Luc Marion, *In Excess: Studies of Saturated Phenomena*, trans. Robyn Horner and Vincent Berraud (New York: Fordham University Press, 2002), pp. 138–139. This same focus on the second negation is present too in his reading of the mystic Denys (Pseudo-Dionysius) in Jean-Luc Marion, *The Idol and Distance: Five Studies*, trans. Thomas A. Carlson (New York: Fordham University Press, 2001).

207   See Jean-Luc Marion, 'The Saturated Phenomenon', *The Visible and the Revealed*, trans. Christina M. Gschwandtner (New York: Fordham University Press, 2008).

The kenotic or impoverished emphasis that Marion places on his rereading of theology as a form of spirituality, and indeed as liturgy, is something that resonates a good deal with other recent phenomenological efforts to more fully detail what a possible 'liturgical reduction' (to parallel Husserl's initial 'phenomenological reduction') might look like.[208] Such is what can be found in the work of Jean-Yves Lacoste, for example, who trains his focus upon how liturgical reduction brackets the experiences of this 'pagan' world (without for that completely doing away with them either) in order to demonstrate the kenotic nature of existence itself. Reading Lacoste's formulations alongside Agamben on the poverty or *kenosis* of ontology also allows the previous political analysis to resonate within the phenomenological in ways that it has not so far. Indeed, the phenomenological is often lacking entirely in a parallel political analysis, though this need not be the case. Such a juxtaposition of the phenomenological and the political, as the genealogists, deconstructivists and critical theorists have already found immensely beneficial, might allow us to appreciate anew something like Antonio Negri's (re)formulation of phenomenology as a collective praxis that depends on poverty and love in order to construct a weak form of sovereignty through the power of the multitude.[209] This is what also led Negri to theorize, along with Michael Hardt, a political form of militant love that took Saint Francis of Assisi as its model.[210] Negri's speculations upon a weak form of sovereignty resonate too with James Mensch's articulation of a kenotic '[...] way to think, not sovereignty as freedom, but rather freedom as sovereignty—that is, sovereignty as the gift of the other' (a point that would not be unfamiliar to Marion's or Derrida's writings on the gift as well).[211]

Alongside such phenomenological formulations, Michel Henry's positing of 'absolute, unique, transcendental, phenomenological Life' that 'gives us access to thought' becomes a proposition that moves the incarnational reality of Life (and, in his estimation, of Christianity's claims about Christ as well) to the forefront of our analysis of the complexities of life itself.[212] Taking up the vital

---

208   See the commentary offered on Marion's work in this regard in Christina M. Gschwandtner, *Marion and Theology* (London: Bloomsbury, 2016).
209   Antonio Negri, *Time for Revolution*, trans. Matteo Mandarini (London: Continuum, 2003).
210   Michael Hardt and Antonio Negri, *Empire* (Cambridge, MA: Harvard University Press, 2001), p. 413.
211   James R. Mensch, *Embodiments: From the Body to the Body Politic* (Evanston, IL: Northwestern University Press, 2009), p. 98. It should be noted too that James Mensch's body politics is worked out in relation to phenomenological trends involving the insights of the Czech phenomenologist Jan Patočka, among others.
212   Michel Henry, *Incarnation: A Philosophy of Flesh*, trans. Karl Hefty (Evanston, IL: Northwestern University Press, 2015), p. 254. See too the more explicitly theological

pulse of life that permeates the theological claims of Christianity, Henry points toward a phenomenology of community that is not limited to humanity alone; rather, we are part of a 'pathetic community' that '[...] includes everything that is defined in itself by the primal suffering of life and thus by the possibility of suffering. We can suffer with everything that suffers. This pathos-with is the broadest form of every conceivable community'.[213] In short, and insofar as it resonates with a certain negative dialectics focused upon suffering, the negation of whatever reductionistic ('negated') identities we have foisted upon each other in order to establish a given logic or rationality is the means by which humanity moves through suffering, and through pathos, to another form of human solidarity—one encountered through what appears to be weakness.

Henry shares in this movement with Elizabeth Grosz's refusal to separate idealism from materiality in order to create a dualistic vision of our world. Rather she affirms a sense of life determined as 'the increasing complexification of material relations' that simultaneously renders conceptual relations that much more complex as well.[214] Such a trend is present as well in Claude Romano's emphasis upon the Husserlian Lebenswelt, or 'life-world', that precedes all forms of knowledge and that was central to Maurice Merleau-Ponty's re-examination of the body's relation to the world.[215] Though speaking only suggestively at this point, I would wager that these phenomenological lines of thought might be merged with Latour's examinations of the complex and various modes of existence, or even Agamben's more recent attempts to develop a modal ontology.[216]

As if speaking directly to the political-theological dualism that I have been considering from the start of the present inquiry, Jacob Rogozinski points toward the manner by which the phenomenological reduction might yet be conceived as an answer to the problematics I have been pursuing throughout this all-too-brief account of continental philosophy. In terms that yet starkly parallel Girard's comments on archaic violence at the foundations of society or Foucault's work on marginalized populations, Rogozinski inclines us

---

resonance in Henry's *I Am the Truth: Toward a Philosophy of Christianity*, trans. Susan Emanuel (Stanford: Stanford University Press, 2003).

213   Michel Henry, *Material Phenomenology*, trans. Scott Davidson (New York: Fordham University Press, 2008), pp. 133–134.

214   Elizabeth Grosz, *The Incorporeal: Ontology, Ethics, and the Limits of Materialism* (New York: Columbia University Press, 2017), p. 251.

215   Claude Romano, *At the Heart of Reason*, trans. Michael B. Smith and Claude Romano (Evanston, IL: Northwestern University Press, 2015), pp. 504–528.

216   Latour, *An Inquiry into the Modes of Existence*, as well as Agamben, *The Use of Bodies*.

to note how it is precisely the phenomenological reduction that opens us up to an experience of the world and its complex relations beyond whatever we had brought to the table.[217] Every identity that was only able to be established through a reductionistic labelling of it, is liberated in order that we might see how it is the exclusion that founds any unity.

> Certainly all the modes of exclusion are not equivalent—but political communities, as different as they are, are constituted in the same manner. Each of them is represented as if it formed only one body, even though its unity is not originary, supposing a more ancient division or the rejection of a heterogeneous element and the denial of foundational violence. If we want to be free of this blindness, of the illusion of the One-Body, we must look for the division that grounds it, the trace of the remainder that it excludes. Only then could we undertaken a radical *epokhè* of the communitarian illusions: only what was dissociated from the Great Body can hope to disclose its hidden truth. For this, we would have to situate *in the place of the remainder* the place of the pariah, the *pharmakôs*, the *homo sacer*, the witch, the heretic, the insane, the proletariat, the *zek*, and all those excluded from the community. More exactly, it would be a matter of making the place of *truth*—wherever the exclusion of the remainder is revealed—coincide with the place of *resistance*, of the subject of action.[218]

Everything is brought to a conclusive head in this evaluation: Agamben's figure of the *homo sacer*, Derrida's *pharmakôs*, Foucault's various marginalized persons, Adorno's focus on Auschwitz, Girard's scapegoat—each of these singular images begins to resonate with their phenomenological counterparts—'Levinas's face, Chrétien's speech, Henry's flesh, Marion's gift, Lacoste's liturgy'. That which was excluded from the normative order, that which does not dwell content within our material reality, becomes that which opens up a new dimension to reality and perhaps the theological, no matter which subfield of continental thought opened us up first to such an insight. It is in such ways, through these reimaginings of phenomenology, that we might be able to go beyond the dualistic impasses that have divided continental philosophy from theology and even certain parts of continental thought from others.

---

217 Jacob Rogozinski, *The Ego and the Flesh: An Introduction to Egoanalysis*, trans. Robert Vallier (Stanford: Stanford University Press, 2010), p. 127.
218 Rogozinski, *The Ego and the Flesh*, pp. 305–306.

Conclusion

It is almost commonplace to assert that the Bible highlights a singular and unique call to assist the marginalized and excluded and that such a call has always been a part of theological discourse, though one often downplayed at times historically when the Church was more aligned with the political powers that be. The force that liberation theology has awakened in our world today is one that we might truly call prophetic in a biblical sense. In this fashion, we might do well to recall too the Jewish theologian Abraham Joshua Heschel's description of the prophetic focus (and especially since this formulation played a significant role in Moltmann's formulation of 'political theology'):

> Since the prophets do not speak in the name of the moral law, it is inaccurate to characterize them as proclaimers of justice, or *mishpat*. It is more accurate to see them as proclaimers of God's pathos, speaking not for the idea of justice, but for the God of justice, for God's concern for justice. Divine concern remembered in sympathy is the stuff of which prophecy is made.[219]

Heschel had sought to develop a 'pathetic' theology that would speak to God's pathos—what he will define as God's 'righteousness wrapped in mystery, togetherness in holy otherness'.[220] The call is not one simply to alleviate all suffering by any means necessary, but to demonstrate how God suffers with those who suffer injustice and oppression; God becomes, in Moltmann's words (and as they echo Luther), the 'crucified God'.

Drawing upon Walter Benjamin's formulation of a 'weak messianic power' moving through history, upending our representations of history in order to bring such images to a standstill and offer oppressed memories the chance to intervene and redirect the course of the future, the political-theologian Johann Baptist Metz has developed a conceptualization of religion 'as interruption' and thereby focused our attention on the 'dangerous memory' of Jesus Christ, the figure who has the power to unseat our given, unjust representations within the present.[221] What such theological formulations offer us today is that which contains a deep resonance with those genealogical-deconstructivist philosophers who would deconstruct Christianity (Nancy), champion

---

219 Abraham Joshua Heschel, *The Prophets* (New York: Harper, 2001), p. 219.
220 Heschel, *The Prophets*, p. 219, de-emphasized from the original.
221 See Johann Baptist Metz, *Faith in History and Society: Toward a Practical Fundamental Theology*, trans. J. Matthew Ashley (New York: Crossroad, 2007).

weak thought in relation to the 'death of God' (Vattimo, Caputo) or attempt to overcome ontotheology (Westphal) in order to reconceive of theology anew. Their 'nihilistic' impulses are thereby revealed as *opportunities* to correct the univocal pronouncements of being (as Desmond put it) in order to arrive at an alternative way to perceive the dualisms that structure life in the western world. What such thinking offers us is a way to proceed toward something like a negative dialectic or phenomenological reduction that pushes us beyond the dualistic limitations in our world without for all of that having to remove dualisms from our world altogether.

I would argue too that Mark Lewis Taylor has already analyzed these dynamics in relation to the field of theology itself in his book *The Theological and the Political* where he considers the dualistic ways in which 'Theology', as a 'guild' discipline (read: sovereign power), is undermined from within by the 'theological', itself a 'weak messianic force' that undoes all the ways in which 'Theology' tries to maintain itself in order to make it a more just system (representation) (read: the liberal-democratic impulse). As he puts it,

> The theological is a discourse that discerns and critically reflects upon the motions of power in this agonistic dimension. More particularly, it traces and theorizes the ways that persons and groups rendered subordinate and vulnerable by agonistic politics and its systemic imposed social suffering nevertheless haunt, unsettle, and perhaps dissolve the structures of those systems. The theological traces and theorizes the way this haunting congeals into specters and forces both threatening and promising alternative patterns and lifeways.[222]

Taylor's proposal is not to look simply toward the material reality in which we live as the only option before us; it is rather a call to examine the 'failed' forms of transcendence that have often diverted us from the proper path.[223] It is only in the failure of an identity—such as what happens in 'Theology' itself then—that we might glimpse the presence of the 'theological' which cannot be identified, but is present nonetheless (precisely what Derrida had also described, alongside Benjamin, as the force of the messianic). It is as such that he seeks to develop an account of our reality, following Nancy, as 'transimmanent', or as 'beyond [the dualism of] transcendence and immanence'[224]—a

---

222 Mark Lewis Taylor, *The Theological and the Political: On the Weight of the World* (Minneapolis, MN: Fortress Press, 2011), p. 9.
223 Taylor, *The Theological and the Political*, p. 23.
224 Taylor, *The Theological and the Political*, p. 152.

conceptualization that perhaps harkens back to Maurice Blondel's 'transnatural' state.[225] This is what the liberation theologian Leonardo Boff elsewhere referred to as the 'interpenetration' of the natural and the supernatural which takes place in such a way as to undo the dualistic tension between them without necessarily jettisoning them as conceptual categories either.[226]

Such tensions as Taylor sees at work in the domain of theology are present in continental thought as well, often in ways that divide scholars from one another in an effort to maintain greater fidelity to the 'original' reading of a text.[227] They divide the phenomenological, at times, from the genealogists and deconstructivists, and they divide the continental philosophical from the theological at the same time, each discourse striving to claim superiority over another, seeking to legitimate some identity over another and marginalizing that which does not make 'sense' within a particular matrix of intelligible representations.

The breakdown in traditional dualistic thinking, however, has been reflected not only in the works of Desmond, Eck, Schrijvers and contemporary phenomenology, but is also being rethought in terms of global forms of governance that are willing to rethink the 'us' versus 'them' mentality,[228] as well as in ways that undermine typical notions of the sovereign self, displacing it through accounts of intersubjectivity.[229] Theology and philosophy are becoming more attentive, especially in their interreligious and comparative fields respectively, to nondualistic ways of conceiving the divine.[230]

What I have tried to demonstrate in the preceding analysis is that continental philosophy, over the last century especially, has called our attention to such dualistic dynamics and impasses, but also possibly our ability to work beyond them in a certain sense, in a profound and illuminating fashion. Perhaps for the first time in human history, we are able to see how specific political,

---

225 Maurice Blondel, *Action: Essay on a Critique of Life and a Science of Practice*, trans. Oliva Blanchette (Notre Dame, IN: University of Notre Dame Press, 1984).

226 Leonardo Boff, *Liberating Grace*, trans. John Drury (Eugene, OR: Wipf & Stock, 2005), p. 45.

227 See, for example, the ways in which Michael Morgan divides Levinas scholars into two camps that very much reflect the dualistic impasse I have been describing between communitarians and genealogical-deconstructivists. Michael L. Morgan, *Levinas's Ethical Politics* (Bloomington, IN: Indiana University Press, 2016).

228 Daniel Innerarity, *Governance in the New Global Disorder: Politics for a Post-Sovereign Society*, trans. Sandra Kingery (New York: Columbia University Press, 2016).

229 Rosine Kelz, *The Non-Sovereign Self, Responsibility, and Otherness: Hannah Arendt, Judith Butler, and Stanley Cavell on Moral Philosophy and Political Agency* (London: Palgrave Macmillan, 2016).

230 See, among others, Milton Scarborough, *Comparative Theories of Nonduality: The Search for a Middle Way* (London: Continuum, 2009).

theological, economic, social and philosophical tensions are not the sign of an unresolved theoretical attempt that needs to be 'straightened out' or resolved once and for all—this was, if anything, the fetish of modernity. They are rather constitutive of each intellectual field—theology and continental philosophy alike—and so unable to go away once and for all. Learning to accept this reality and to creatively deal with the situation that such impasses present us with is the task for the futures of both continental philosophy and theology, and it is one that is not a moment too soon in coming.

Bibliography

Primary Texts

Theodor W. Adorno, *Negative Dialectics*, trans. E.B. Ashton, London: Continuum, 1973.

> Along with his *Minima Moralia: Reflections On a Damaged Life*, trans. E.F.N. Jephcott (London: Verso, 2006), Adorno's *Negative Dialectics* stands as a monumental resource to both philosophers and theologians. His influence upon the origins of modern political and liberation theologies has been noted, and continues to be a point of departure for theologians looking to explore how the 'negation of negation' plays out in philosophical terms. Along with this magnum opus, Adorno's co-authored study with Max Horkheimer, their *Dialectic of Enlightenment*, ed. Gunzelin Schmid Noerr, trans. Edmund Jephcott (Stanford: Stanford University Press, 2007) remains another central text that seeks to demythologize the culture (economically and politically) in which we live.

Giorgio Agamben, *The Time that Remains: A Commentary on the Letter to the Romans*, trans. Patricia Dailey, Stanford: Stanford University Press, 2005.

> Though his *Homo Sacer* series is perhaps most deserving of study for the ways in which it prompts us to rethink the political and theological boundaries of exclusion and how we might live a form-of-life beyond all forms of law, it is *The Time that Remains* which meticulously unfolds the Pauline influence Agamben senses latent behind much of philosophical thought (including the work of Walter Benjamin, one of his most significant sources of insight). In many ways, Agamben's close reading of Paul's Letter to the Romans, which this book deftly inspects, is the key to reading the rest of the *Homo Sacer* series and discerning what Agamben is really putting forth through the series as his contribution to philosophical inquiry.

Alain Badiou, *Saint Paul: The Foundation of Universalism*, trans. Ray Brassier, Stanford: Stanford University Press, 2003.

> Though the larger portion of his major philosophical writings lie in other domains of thought, Badiou's short study of the Pauline corpus has been central to understanding his philosophy on the whole, as well as the varied 'returns to religion' within continental thought. The militant subject of universality that this committed atheist and communist reads within the writings of Saint Paul is profoundly illuminating with regards to the political and social nature of the earliest forms of Christianity.

Walter Benjamin, 'Critique of Violence', *Selected Writings*, vol. 1, ed. Marcus Bullock and Michael W. Jennings, trans. Edmund Jephcott et al., Cambridge, MA: Harvard University Press, 1996.

> Along with a variety of essays and fragments that speak directly to the theological, including his much celebrated theses 'On the Concept of History' that unfurls his notion of a 'weak messianic force', as well as his more theoretical reflections in his *Arcades Project*, Benjamin's much earlier essay 'Critique of Violence' introduces us to the possibility of thinking outside of or beyond the political structures we have before us, even being so bold as to claim there is a way to enact 'divine violence' through the suspension of normative relations. Benjamin's work is only now beginning to get the attention it deserves from its theological readers, and one should hope that many more scholars begin to pay attention to such a trend.

Pierre Bourdieu, *Language and Symbolic Power*, ed. John B. Thompson, trans. Gino Raymond and Matthew Adamson, Cambridge, MA: Harvard University Press, 1991.

> The resonance between Pierre Bourdieu's study of symbolic power and much of what has gone on in contemporary continental thought, especially regarding power within theological and ecclesial contexts, is widely overlooked, though this should be anything but the case. In this book, we find a well-reasoned argument for how power is embedded in the discourses that sustain much of what has been considered as theological conversation—a point that many today would do well to pay closer attention to. For an exemplary case study of how these dynamics are played out socially, we might look further to his *Masculine Domination*, trans. Richard Nice (Stanford: Stanford University Press, 2001).

Stanislas Breton, *A Radical Philosophy of Saint Paul*, trans. Joseph N. Ballan, New York: Columbia University Press, 2011.

> Along with his *The Word and the Cross*, trans. Jacquelyn Porter (New York: Fordham University Press, 2002), *A Radical Philosophy of Saint Paul* presents us with the stunning abilities of Breton's work to contemplate the Christian legacy from a continental point of view. In this book, Breton finds a way to link the dissolution of identity as found in Pauline thought with the inoperativity of the powers of this world and the establishment of hermeneutical philosophy—points that make this study one in synch with a good many other contemporary returns to Saint Paul.

John D. Caputo, *The Weakness of God: A Theology of the Event*, Bloomington, IN: Indiana University Press, 2006.

> Though there is a good deal of overlap between this book and his later *The Insistence of God: A Theology of Perhaps* (Bloomington, IN: Indiana University Press, 2013), it is in *The Weakness of God* that we first see Caputo's more openly theological engagement with the Christian narrative and deconstructivist thought more generally. His call for a kenotic weakening of thought based on the 'weak messianic power' to be found inherent in all representations, even the religious ones, offers up a hope in the impossible possible or possible impossible that may be beyond all ability to name it, though its hold upon us is not lessened. In many ways, what we see in *The Weakness of God* is really the unfolding of an argument concerning the writings of the philosopher Jacques Derrida that he had worked out most fully in his earlier *The Prayers and Tears of Jacques Derrida: Religion without Religion* (Bloomington, IN: Indiana University Press, 1997).

Gilles Deleuze and Félix Guattari, *What Is Philosophy?*, trans. Hugh Tomlinson and Graham Burchell, New York: Columbia University Press, 1994.

> Anything but an introductory text, their collaborative effort in *What Is Philosophy?* builds from previous ones in order to detail an exposition of a form of immanence beyond the traditional dualism of transcendence/immanence. In addition, it is in their *A Thousand Plateaus: Capitalism and Schizophrenia*, trans. Brian Massumi (Minneapolis, MN: University of Minnesota Press, 1987) that we begin to see an exposition of rhizomatic structures dictate a completely different methodology of inquiry than had been previously imagined, and providing much fuel for a theological thinking that wishes not to build upon foundational

logics, but to expand toward the complex interactions that, more realistically, comprise the structures of our world.

Jacques Derrida, *Of Grammatology*, trans. Gayatri Chakravorty Spivak, Baltimore, MD: Johns Hopkins University Press, 1976.

> The discussion of an impossible presentation of the thing itself beyond all forms of representation toward the end of the book offers us indirectly a profound meditation on the conditions of any potential apophatic theology, something that Derrida later took up directly in much the same way in his *On the Name*, ed. Thomas Dutoit, trans. David Wood (Stanford: Stanford University Press, 1995). The basic coordinates of language and representation that he took up in *Of Grammatology* then reappear in relation to the messianic in his later *Specters of Marx: The State of the Debt, the Work of Mourning and the New International*, trans. Peggy Kamuf (London: Routledge, 1994), the reading of which allows us to sense too why the issues of justice and hospitality, two highly religious themes, appear so pronounced in his later writings.

William Desmond, *God and the Between*, Oxford: Blackwell, 2008.

> Though perhaps lesser known than many other continental thinkers, Desmond's highly original philosophical work on the porosity of our being allows us to rethink the excessive, hyperbolic nature of existence as it points us toward that which lies beyond us. Though very dense in its rigorous argumentation and somewhat idiosyncratic in its terminology, Desmond's *God and the Between* provides us with a *metaxological* sense of existing in an 'overdetermined' way, hence directed by our existence toward that which exceeds it. In many ways, Desmond's work provides us with a philosophical ground so convincing it has been endorsed by thinkers as diverse as John Caputo and John Milbank alike.

Terry Eagleton, *Reason, Faith, and Revolution: Reflections on the God Debate*, New Haven, CT: Yale University Press, 2009.

> Staking his ground amongst recent debates regarding popular forms of atheism, Eagleton is able to demonstrate how such positions are embedded much deeper in modern sentiments than many might suspect, as well as how dismissive such positions are toward the reality of religious faith. In this work and in his subsequent *Culture and the Death of God* (New Haven, CT: Yale University Press, 2014) and *Hope without Optimism* (Charlottesville, VA: University of Virginia Press,

2015), Eagleton maneuvers through a variety of literary and theoretical sources in order to pursue the relevance of religious and theological claims, somewhat too in the vein of Charles Taylor's work on secularization.

Emmanuel Falque, *Crossing the Rubicon: The Borderlands of Philosophy and Theology*, trans. Reuben Shank and Matthew Farley, New York: Fordham University Press, 2016.

In addition to his *The Metamorphosis of Finitude: An Essay on Birth and Resurrection*, trans. George Hughes (New York: Fordham University Press, 2012), *Crossing the Rubicon* makes an argument for the porousness of the borders between philosophy and theology, as well as the boundaries between hermeneutics and phenomenology. The strength of Falque's analysis lies primarily in his ability to merge so many different strains of philosophical thought with the history of theology, something that allows this work to be a very timely contribution to contemporary and ongoing debates concerning the various interactions of each of these fields of thought.

Michel Foucault, *Security, Territory, Population: Lectures at the Collège de France, 1977–1978*, ed. Michel Senellart, trans. Graham Burchell, New York: Picador, 2007.

The publication of Foucault's lectures has brought a plurality of (mainly western) theological issues to the fore of his thought, much of which is still being subjected to further scholarly inquiry at the moment. What these lectures in particular, along with his *On the Government of the Living: Lectures at the Collège de France, 1979–1980*, ed. Michel Senellart, trans. Graham Burchell (New York: Palgrave Macmillan, 2014) and *The Hermeneutics of the Subject: Lectures at the Collège de France, 1981–1982*, ed. Frédéric Gros, trans. Graham Burchell (New York: Picador, 2005) bring to light is the way in which the history of Christianity, its ecclesial exercises of pastoral power, confession and penance, as well as its internal mystical resistance to such forces, lies not only at the center of theological work, but at the center of Foucault's own thought as well.

René Girard, *I See Satan Fall Like Lightning*, trans. James G. Williams, Maryknoll, NY: Orbis, 2004.

René Girard's work has become inescapable in terms of comprehending the significance of the sweeping scope and major claims that his work on victimhood, scapegoating, biblical and mythological narratives, violence and exclusion presents us with. In *I See Satan Fall Like Lightning*, as well as *The Scapegoat*, trans. Yvonne Freccero (Baltimore, MD: Johns Hopkins University Press, 1989) and his interview-based study, *Things Hidden Since the Foundation of the World*, trans. Stephen Bann and Michael Metteer (Stanford: Stanford University Press, 1987), Girard's thought is portrayed as vital to the heart of both theology and philosophy (as in his profound readings of Nietzsche). If there is truth to his reading of selected historical texts, then the entire enterprise of western thought (and religion) must be rethought anew, and in terms that take more seriously how humanity seems to ceaselessly repeat its imitative (mimetic) acts of scapegoating in order to ensure a (false) sense of peace is restored to communal life.

Martin Heidegger, *The Phenomenology of Religious Life*, trans. Matthias Fritsch and Jennifer Anna Gosetti-Ferencei, Bloomington, IN: Indiana University Press, 2010.

Demonstrating that the contemporary returns to Saint Paul were already being contemplated in the early 20th Century, Heidegger's lectures on *The Phenomenology of Religious Life* point toward a number of claims resonant with later thought, but also highly illuminative of the steps that his own writing would take after these lectures, as, for example, in his most significant work, *Being and Time*, trans. Joan Stambaugh (rev. ed., Albany, NY: State University of New York Press, 2010). As Heidegger's work continues to be debated and discussed (especially in light of his anti-Semitic remarks in his so-called 'black notebooks'), it is incumbent upon scholars to study further his interpretations of Christianity.

Michel Henry, *I Am the Truth: Toward a Philosophy of Christianity*, trans. Susan Emanuel, Stanford: Stanford University Press, 2003.

The phenomenology of Henry points us toward a material theology that can be most directly accessed in both his *I Am the Truth* and in his *Incarnation: A Philosophy of Flesh*, trans. Karl Hefty (Evanston, IL: Northwestern University Press, 2015). The truth that Henry attempts to present in this work in particular is the one that Christianity itself presents through its teachings and traditions, an embodied truth that points us beyond the world's economies and towards a radical poverty of the self.

Edmund Husserl, *The Crisis of European Sciences and Transcendental Phenomenology: An Introduction to Phenomenological Philosophy*, trans. David Carr, Evanston, IL: Northwestern University Press, 1970.

This book has been credited with saving philosophy after the incompletions of Heidegger's *Being and Time*. As radical as such a claim might sound, Husserl undertakes here another study of his most fundamental concepts, yet broadening his approach to include the way in which our being fundamentally intersubjective beings means that the self is not an isolated phenomena, but is one rather that comprehends itself in the midst of a world of subjects. So much of contemporary phenomenology begins its investigations here.

Luce Irigaray, *The Way of Love*, trans. Heidi Bostic and Stephen Pluháček, London: Continuum, 2002.

The wonderful Luce Irigaray offers us a short, but powerful work on the ways in which western philosophical thought has lost the path when it comes to discussions of love, a point that even Alain Badiou has not been ignorant of in recent memory. Her willingness to consider the nature of love from a feminist point of view opens up our understanding of what stretches beyond thought, while also reaching into the very foundations of thought. In this way, she develops a philosophical meditation that takes part in her later spiritual writings as well.

Dominique Janicaud, et al., *Phenomenology and the Theological Turn: The French Debate*, New York: Fordham University Press, 2001.

The book that in many ways inspired a critical look at what had already been going on for some time in French phenomenology, Dominique Janicaud's study of the 'theological turn' provides major criticisms of this alleged 'turn' while also demonstrating quite remarkably the significance that such authors hold for phenomenological thought on the whole. Janicaud's essays constitute the first part of the volume, and multiple responses—from Jean-François Courtine, Ricoeur, Chrétien, Marion and Henry—constitute the second part.

Richard Kearney, *Anatheism: Returning to God After God*, New York: Columbia University Press, 2011.

Somewhere between theism and atheism, Richard Kearney locates an anatheism capable of rejuvenating our theological appetites in creative dialogue with philosophers, poets and theologians alike. Bold in scope and comprehensive in coverage, Kearney evolves his earlier wagers concerning *The God Who May Be: A Hermeneutics of Religion* (Bloomington, IN: Indiana University Press, 2001) in order to portray the role of the ultimate 'Other' in our world. In his subsequent *Reimagining the Sacred: Richard Kearney Debates God*, eds. Richard Kearney and Jens Zimmermann (New York: Columbia University Press, 2016) Kearney takes up a series of conversations between himself and numerous theologians and philosophers, many of whom have been discussed in the present study. The conversations are generally mutually appreciative explorations of speech about God 'after God', and the conversational tone provides a helpful introduction to some themes in contemporary continental philosophy of religion.

Jean-Yves Lacoste, *Experience and the Absolute: Disputed Questions on the Humanity of Man*, trans. Mark Raftery-Skehan, New York: Fordham University Press, 2004.

> Jean-Yves Lacoste's embrace of the affective side of human existence as that which must be in dialogue with any form of knowing (hence his siding, at times, with Schleiermacher's emphasis on feeling over Hegel's sense of absolute knowledge) allows Lacoste to rethink the relationship of phenomenology to theology, and often in provocative and profound ways. Allowing there to be a porousness between experience and knowledge, in turn, Lacoste imagines a kenotic way of being in the world that he finds mirrored in certain theological, even mystical, ways of being in the world. This book is a subtle and essential contribution to contemporary phenomenological conversations.

Philippe Lacoue-Labarthe, *Poetry as Experience*, trans. Andrea Tarnowski, Stanford: Stanford University Press, 1999.

> This short meditation on the poetry of Paul Celan becomes a much larger and creative investigation into the ways forward for prayer in an a/theological age. Though our words seem to be emptied of all content in a post-Auschwitz world of suffering, one that Celan knew from his own experiences of loss during the Second World War all-too-well, Lacoue-Labarthe argues that there is yet something to be found in crying out to the 'no one' whom Celan's poems frequently address.

Bruno Latour, *An Inquiry into Modes of Existence: An Anthropology of the Moderns*, trans. Catherine Porter, Cambridge, MA: Harvard University Press, 2013.

> Though perhaps more well-known is his *We Have Never Been Modern*, trans. Catherine Porter (Cambridge, MA: Harvard University Press, 1993), *An Inquiry into Modes of Existence* is a much fuller exposition of Latour's philosophy, one developed not as a separate exercise in philosophical rigor, but as a thinking of the networks and interconnections that exist between a variety of the modes of existence in our world, including politics, science, literature, art, religion and economics, to name but some of the modes he investigates from an anthropological point of view. The interconnectedness of all things brings his analysis to the fore of an ecological way of being in the world, and, considering the times we

live in, there may not be a more relevant perspective for us to find a way forward. In addition to his remarks on religion in this volume, his more overt essay on religious speech, *Rejoicing: Or, the Torments of Religious Speech*, trans. Julie Rose (Cambridge: Polity, 2013) is well-worth reading, as it explores the ways we typically make category mistakes in assigning religious tasks to non-religious modes and vice versa.

Emmanuel Levinas, *Otherwise than Being, or Beyond Essence*, trans. Alphonso Lingis, Pittsburgh, PA: Duquesne University Press, 1998.

Levinas' magisterial study of otherness and being has prompted nothing less than a full scale re-examination of phenomenology in relation to ethics, going beyond Heidegger's claims that ontology is the bedrock of all philosophical thought and opening us up toward a more relational approach, one rooted in the face of the other standing before us and making demands upon us. Building off of his earlier *Totality and Infinity: An Essay on Exteriority*, trans. Alphonso Lingis (Pittsburgh, PA: Duquesne University Press, 1969), his *Otherwise than Being* offers us a rereading of religious themes in our world, and often in provocative and startling ways.

Jean-François Lyotard, *The Differend: Phrases in Dispute*, trans. Georges Van Den Abbeele, Minneapolis, MN: University of Minnesota Press, 1988.

Though his writings on postmodernity often draw the most attention, it is Lyotard's *The Differend* which truly displays the vast scope of thought his work was capable of engaging. Not only is this work one of the last century's great philosophical and linguistic treatises, it is also one that points toward an understanding of the Christian narrative as an open narrative that is capable of retaining a sense of self-critical understanding. Few theologians—Lieven Boeve notably among them—have grasped the significance of Lyotard's thought for theology today, and it is my hope that many more might access his work in order to flush out what else of significance it still holds for us.

Catherine Malabou, *Plasticity at the Dusk of Writing: Dialectic, Destruction, Deconstruction*, trans. Carolyn Shread, New York: Columbia University Press, 2009.

The work of Catherine Malabou has drawn increasing attention as of late, mainly through the readings of Clayton Crockett, Jeffrey Robbins and Ward Blanton, as she is able to point toward a fundamental state of existence rooted in a concept of change that, so she claims, precedes the Derridean emphasis on différance.

By further developing Hegel's notion of plasticity, something she has brought into dialogue at times with neuroscience, Malabou's work offers us a refreshingly unique point of view that is increasingly being listened to by continental philosophers of religion.

Jean-Luc Marion, *The Visible and the Revealed*, trans. Christina Gschwandtner, New York: Fordham University Press, 2008.

The work of Jean-Luc Marion has, for decades now, consistently pointed toward the resonance of various theological themes within contemporary phenomenology. *The Visible and the Revealed*, in particular, does a good job of isolating some of the biggest themes he takes up—givenness and the gift, potentiality, revelation, the saturated phenomenon and the possibility of a Christian philosophy—all in a very accessible and comprehensive manner, making this collection a good introduction to his thought on the whole. In addition, his *In Excess: Studies of Saturated Phenomena*, trans. Robyn Horner and Vincent Berraud (New York: Fordham University Press, 2004) and, more substantially, *Being Given: Toward a Phenomenology of Givenness*, trans. Jeffrey L. Kosky (Stanford: Stanford University Press, 2002) also bring the reader to an encounter with the way in which Marion's work has set a new course for phenomenological and hermeneutical thought in our day.

Jean-Luc Nancy, *Dis-Enclosure: The Deconstruction of Christianity*, trans. Bettina Bergo, Gabriel Malenfant and Michael B. Smith, New York: Fordham University Press, 2008.

Jean-Luc Nancy's work follows somewhat in the footsteps of Derrida's deconstructive acts, and yet it has taken an increasingly visible turn toward the history of Christianity and what its possible deconstruction might yield for philosophical thought in general. Along with *Dis-Enclosure*, Nancy's subsequent *Adoration: The Deconstruction of Christianity II*, trans. John McKeane (New York: Fordham University Press, 2013) and *Noli me tangere: On the Raising of the Body*, trans. Sarah Clift, Pascale-Anne Brault and Michael Naas (New York: Fordham University Press, 2008) provide an alternative route by which to contemplate the legacy of Christian thought in a secular age.

Paul Ricoeur, *The Rule of Metaphor: The Creation of Meaning in Language*, trans. Robert Czerny, Kathleen McLaughlin and John Costello, London: Routledge, 1977.

It has been argued that Ricoeur's *The Rule of Metaphor* is, and remains, his central work. I find no reason to diverge from this opinion, and his analysis of the analogy of being in relation to metaphor and the history of ontotheology is second to none. Taken together with his work on memory and history, *Memory, History, Forgetting*, trans. Kathleen Blamey and David Pellauer (Chicago: University of Chicago Press, 2004) and the collection of essays gathered as *Figuring the Sacred: Religion, Narrative, and Imagination*, trans. David Pellauer, ed. Mark I. Wallace (Minneapolis, MN: Fortress Press, 1995), we can discern in Ricoeur's writings some major theological lines of thought that contain a great degree of significance for contemporary philosophers of religion.

Jacob Taubes, *The Political Theology of Paul*, trans. Dana Hollander, Stanford: Stanford University Press, 2003.

Capturing what many have considered to be the start of the many 'returns' to Saint Paul's thought, Jacob Taubes' last series of lectures before his death bring a renewed reading of Pauline thought to bear on contemporary philosophical issues, allowing us to sense the long lineage from these scriptural letters to Nietzsche and Freud in particular. His reading of Gershom Scholem and Sabbati Zevi in relation to Paul and possible antinomian thought make this short study further a remarkable one.

Gianni Vattimo, *After Christianity*, trans. Luca D'Isanto, New York: Columbia University Press, 2002.

Taking up a very interesting position as someone who has returned to his Catholic roots via Nietzsche, Heidegger and even René Girard, Vattimo's championing of 'weak thought' overlaps a good deal with that of John Caputo, though the way in which he honestly confronts Christian themes from a philosophical perspective contains its own unique twists and turns. Much of this is captured in a somewhat autobiographical form in his short book *Belief*, trans. Luca D'Isanto and David Webb (Stanford: Stanford University Press, 1999).

Merold Westphal, *Postmodern Philosophy and Christian Thought*, Bloomington, IN: Indiana University Press, 1999.

Merold Westphal has cemented his reputation as a major conversant in the field and this initial study of what a postmodern theology might resemble certainly announced his arrival in many ways. Subsequent studies, such as his *Overcoming Onto-Theology: Toward a Postmodern Christian Faith* (New York: Fordham

University Press, 2001) and *Transcendence and Self-Transcendence: On God and the Soul* (Bloomington, IN: Indiana University Press, 2004) likewise dared readers to consider what new forms of theological thinking were going to be necessary in an age where doctrine is not as substantial as it had once appeared to be.

Slavoj Žižek, *Less Than Nothing: Hegel and the Shadow of Dialectical Materialism*, London: Verso, 2013.

My intuition is that Žižek's *Less Than Nothing* is the current 'magnum opus' within his corpus, and this despite the fact that he has himself frequently issued pronouncements on the canonical status of his own works. In this one we find a sustained engagement with a variety of theological themes in relation to his thought on the whole, hence Hegel and Lacan are brought into dialogue once again with Christian themes, though in a way that clarifies a good deal of his previoius work. There is no doubt that earlier writings by Žižek on Christianity are still beneficial to study, however, including his *The Fragile Absolute: Or, Why Is the Christian Legacy Worth Fighting For?* (London: Verso, 2000), *On Belief* (London: Routledge, 2001) and *The Puppet and the Dwarf: The Perverse Core of Christianity* (Cambridge, MA: MIT Press, 2003).

Secondary Texts
Tina Beattie, *Theology after Postmodernity: Divining the Void—A Lacanian Reading of Thomas Aquinas*, Oxford: Oxford University Press, 2013.

Tina Beattie offers critical and constructive readings of both Jacques Lacan and Aquinas in relation to contemporary philosophers of religion (including, most prominently, Caputo and Kearney). She utilizes Lacan to explore and critique the gendered theology of Aquinas and to construct a theology of desire that draws on some of Thomas' own work as well as on the mystical tradition. In so doing she also provides a reevaluation of Lacan's own secularized Thomism.

Bruce Ellis Benson and Norman Wirzba, eds., *The Phenomenology of Prayer*, New York: Fordham University Press, 2005.

Authors from various religious perspectives write on how prayer and phenomenology relate to one another, and on the phenomenology of religious experience more generally. In addition to Benson and Wirzba, contributors include Philip Goodchild, Lissa McCullough, and Merold Westphal.

Bruce Ellis Benson and Norman Wirzba, eds., *Transforming Philosophy and Religion: Love's Wisdom*, Indiana Series in Philosophy of Religion, Bloomington: Indiana University Press, 2008.

> Taking its departure from Levinas' redefinition of philosophy as the wisdom of love, this collection of essays is divided into sections exploring love's impact on philosophy, justice, sacrality, and anthropology. In addition to Wirzba and Benson, authors include John D. Caputo, Christina Gschwandtner, James Olthuis, and Brian Treanor.

Bruce Ellis Benson and Norman Wirzba, eds., *Words of Life: New Theological Turns in French Phenomenology*, New York: Fordham University Press, 2010.

> A companion to Janicaud et. al.'s *Phenomenology and the Theological Turn*, this volume addresses its predecessor's concerns with the question of whether or not theology can be properly phenomenological, yet goes beyond this launching point in treating several theological-philosophical themes as well as the phenomenology of religious practices.

Ward Blanton and Hent de Vries, eds., *Paul and the Philosophers*, New York: Fordham University Press, 2013.

> This rather large volume examines the turn to Paul in diverse strands of contemporary philosophy, and it does so remarkably well. In particular, there are noteworthy essays included that help to contextualize this philosophical trend, by Paul Ricoeur, Slavoj Žižek, Alain Badiou, Gilles Deleuze, Roland Boer, Clayton Crockett, Simon Critchley, Gil Anidjar, Eleanor Kaufman, Kenneth Reinhard and Hent de Vries, among many others.

Jeffrey Bloechl, ed., *Religious Experience and the End of Metaphysics*, Bloomington: Indiana University Press, 2003.

> Including essays by Adriaan Peperzak and Kevin Hart, this collection examines philosophy and theology after Heidegger's critique of ontotheology, making this an eminently suitable study for those interested in seeing how the supposed 'end of metaphysics' has come to dominate much reflection on the state of contemporary continental thought.

Phillip Blond, ed., *Post-Secular Philosophy: Between Philosophy and Theology*, London: Routledge, 1998.

Blond provides a thorough introduction which is followed by essays on major thinkers in the Continental tradition, placing these thinkers in their historical and philosophical contexts and examining how the theological is encountered in their work. Contributions include essays on Descartes (Jean-Luc Marion), Kant (Howard Caygill), Hegel (Rowan Williams), Kierkegaard (John Milbank), Marion (Graham Ward) and Derrida (Kevin Hart), among others.

Lieven Boeve and Christophe Brabant, eds., *Between Philosophy and Theology: Contemporary Interpretations of Christianity*, Farnham: Ashgate, 2010.

Based on a series of seminars offered at the Catholic University of Leuven (Belgium), this collection of essays does an excellent job in situating continental thought in relation to theological trends. Topics included the work of Richard Kearney, John Caputo, Jean-Luc Nancy, Graham Ward, Michel de Certeau, William Desmond, René Girard, Ellen Armour, Gianni Vattimo and Alain Badiou. Contributors include Caputo, Ward, Desmond, Kevin Hart, Lieven Boeve, Frederiek Depoortere, Joeri Schrijvers and Ellen Armour, among others.

John D. Caputo, *Philosophy and Theology*, Nashville, TN: Abingdon Press, 2006.

In this brief but compelling work, Caputo outlines the history of the increasingly contentious relationship of philosophy to theology, arguing that they ask many of the same questions and must continue to be in conversation in the postmodern age. As such, this book makes for a very readable introduction to the field in many ways.

John D. Caputo, ed., *The Religious, Blackwell Readings in Continental Philosophy*, Oxford: Blackwell, 2001.

In addition to several new essays, this book is a collection of important texts in philosophy, especially whatever we are to consider as continental philosophy *after* metaphysics. Included are works from Kierkegaard, Heidegger, Levinas, Derrida, and Irigaray.

John D. Caputo and Linda Martín Alcoff, eds., *St. Paul Among the Philosophers*, Bloomington, IN: Indiana University Press, 2009.

This volume focuses on the 'new Paul' that has arisen in continental thought, giving attention to how both Christian and atheist philosophers, notably Alain Badiou, have recently taken up Paul's themes of universalism and on the implications of Paul for philosophy, including political philosophy. Alain Badiou, Slavoj Žižek, E.P. Sanders, and Daniel Boyarin are among the contributors.

John D. Caputo, Mark Dooley, and Michael J. Scanlon, eds., *Questioning God*, Bloomington: Indiana University Press, 2001.

This volume stems from a conversation between Jacques Derrida and theologians and philosophers on forgiveness and on God, making a significant contribution toward our understanding of the primacy of forgiveness as a philosophical concept. Contributors include Derrida, Caputo, Richard Kearney, Jean Greisch, John Milbank, Graham Ward, Francis Schüssler Fiorenza, and others.

Simon Critchley, *The Faith of the Faithless: Experiments in Political Theology*, London: Verso, 2014.

Simon Critchley provides much needed commentary on contemporary trends in continental interest in religion, calling for an 'atheistic faith' while noting too that political philosophy is theological language in a different register, a 'metamorphos[i]s of sacralisation'. For Critchley, politics is religious, and thus an atheistic 'faith' is necessary for political action. Critchley positions his reading of such a faith against the political philosophy of Slavoj Žižek.

Clayton Crockett and B. Keith Putt, eds., *The Future of Continental Philosophy of Religion*, Bloomington, IN: Indiana University Press, 2014.

These essays are organized around three central thematic nodes: the messianic (with special attention to the work of John D. Caputo), liberation (with special attention to Philip Goodchild), and plasticity (taking up the interesting work of Catherine Malabou). Through the efforts of this book, postmodern philosophy is brought into conversation with political theology, neuroscience, and evolutionary psychology in substantial and significant ways.

Conor Cunningham and Peter M. Candler, Jr., *Transcendence and Phenomenology*, London: SCM Press, 2007.

This volume presents us with a collection of essays on the concept of transcendence in recent phenomenological thought, including ones by Michel Henry, Jean-Yves Lacoste, Simon Critchley, Philipp Rosemann, John Milbank and Richard Kearney. Authors largely engage the late Michel Henry's work. The volume represents a close relationship between philosophical and theological thought.

Colby Dickinson, ed., *The Postmodern Saints of France*, London: T&T Clark, 2013.

> This volume takes up the question of how our varied notions of saintliness are reconceived by a variety of French intellectuals, providing some intriguing perspectives and twists on an otherwise familiar topic. Each French author is treated by a commentator in the field, with contributions on Jean Genet (Colby Dickinson), Levinas (Michael Purcell), Blanchot (Kevin Hart), Foucault (Ward Blanton), Deleuze (Clayton Crockett), Derrida (Robyn Horner), Laruelle (Anthony Paul Smith) and many others.

Philip Goodchild, ed., *Rethinking Philosophy of Religion: Approaches from Continental Philosophy*, New York: Fordham University Press, 2002.

> After an introduction framing continental philosophy of religion, both its history and its current directions, the following sections interrogate where reason may be located and how this relates to theology and religion. Chapter authors include John D. Caputo, Bettina Bergo, Graham Ward, Edith Wyschogrod and Clayton Crockett.

Christina M. Gschwandtner, *Postmodern Apologetics? Arguments for God in Contemporary Philosophy*, New York: Fordham University Press, 2013.

> Christina Gschwandtner, a prominent commentator of contemporary phenomenological trends, argues that such thinkers as Ricoeur, Marion, Henry, Chrétien, Lacoste, Falque, Westphal, Caputo, and Kearney are all, in a certain sense, 'apologists' for Christianity—not in the traditional sense of offering proofs of God's existence, but in a weaker sense as articulating some measure of meaning and purpose to Christianity. In so arguing she also provides a valuable introduction to these thinkers.

Kevin Hart, *Kingdoms of God*, Bloomington, IN: Indiana University Press, 2014.

> Kevin Hart, a leading light in the field, gives us a 'phenomenology of Christ' in which the multiplicity of interpretations of Jesus Christ yield multiple kingdoms of God. This connected series of essays takes up the central themes of Christology and Trinity, in particular, arguing that phenomenology can be a theological enterprise and that Christ himself was in some sense a phenomenologist.

Kevin Hart and Barbara Wall, eds., *The Experience of God: A Postmodern Response*, New York: Fordham University Press, 2005.

The question uniting the papers in this volume, notably including essays by John D. Caputo, Kristine Culp, Jean-Yves Lacoste, Kevin Hart, and Michael Purcell, is: in what sense is it possible for human beings to have an experience of God? It cannot be the case that God is experienced in the way that material objects are, and so much work is still needing to be done in understanding human perception. The essays examine this question in phenomenological, feminist, and theological perspectives.

Morny Joy, ed., *Continental Philosophy and Philosophy of Religion*, vol. 4 of *Handbook of Contemporary Philosophy of Religion*, New York: Springer, 2011.

A survey of twentieth-century continental philosophy of religion, with the stated purpose of contributing to Anglophone conversations on philosophy of religion. Includes substantial chapters on Ricoeur, Levinas, Kristeva and Irigaray, Foucault, Deleuze, and Marion. Contributors include Joy, Christina M. Gschwandtner, and Bettina Bergo, in addition to many others.

Gregg Lambert, *Return Statements: The Return of Religion in Contemporary Philosophy*, Edinburgh: Edinburgh University Press, 2016.

Lambert examines both the theological turn in philosophy alongside the postsecular turn in contemporary society though from a lens perhaps more critical of this perceived turn than most, therefore, in my opinion, very worthy of listening to. He focuses specifically on the work of Badiou, Caputo, Derrida, and Nancy, among others.

Eugene Thomas Long, ed., *Self and Other: Essays in Continental Philosophy of Religion*, Dordrecht: Springer, 2007.

Long introduces the field through its major themes, and the book as a whole does a decent job of presenting the significance of the various movements identified in the volume: the "other", historicity, the problem of evil, and the relationship of philosophy to theology. Includes essays by Hent de Vries, Pamela Sue Anderson, and Merold Westphal, among others.

Karmen MacKendrick, *Divine Enticement: Theological Seductions*, New York: Fordham University Press, 2013.

Much like Caputo's work in many ways, Karmen MacKendrick envisions theology as a form of speech that seduces, beckons and entices, rather than dogmatically pronounce its views. In this, she shares much with those who contemplate the theo-poetic and she deals with many postmodern and premodern thinkers (her main interlocutor here being Augustine) in order to explore other ways to contemplate the tasks and relevance of theological thought.

John Panteleimon Manoussakis, ed., *After God: Richard Kearney and the Religious Turn in Continental Philosophy*, New York: Fordham University Press, 2006.

The essays in this volume respond to the work of Richard Kearney and so make for invaluable reading in order to grasp the significance of Kearney's work for the fields of continental thought and theology. Includes essays by John D. Caputo, Catherine Keller, David Tracy, and Sallie McFague, among others.

Felix Ó Murchadha, *A Phenomenology of Christian Life: Glory and Night*, Bloomington, IN: Indiana University Press, 2013.

Against the claim (made by Janicaud) that the theological turn betrays Husserlian phenomenology by focusing on the invisible, Ó Murchadha argues that the 'dark night' is, rather than simply a lack (as envisioned by Greek philosophy and, inadvertently, by other philosophers as well), a phenomenon in and of itself, one that must be examined from a religious phenomenological perspective.

James H. Olthuis, ed., *Religion With/out Religion: The Prayers and tears of John D. Caputo*, London: Routledge, 2002.

The volume consists of a series of essays crafted in response to Caputo's *The Prayers and Tears of Jacques Derrida*, a major intervention in relations between deconstructionism and theological impulses, and concludes with a significant response by Caputo himself.

George Pattison, *God and Being: An Enquiry*, Oxford: Oxford University Press, 2011.

This study raises questions that arise generally out of the critique of identifying God with Being, and points, along with several other recent interpreters, toward something like an ontology of poverty or a 'weak' form of thought that is in need of further consideration. Pattison's study is not for the beginner, but is a steady and reliable guide in gaining a comprehension of the field as a whole.

Adriaan Theodoor Peperzak, *Philosophy Between Faith and Theology: Addresses to Catholic Intellectuals*, Notre Dame, IN: University of Notre Dame Press, 2005.

This collection of essays by a major Catholic continental thinker consists of two parts: in the first, Peperzak examines how one might be a Catholic intellectual, and specifically a Catholic philosopher, including his asking of particular questions, such as: what role does Christianity play in the academy and in the discipline of philosophy? What questions with particular theological resonance (such as, for example, desire) have been ignored by philosophy? The second part engages particular topics such as prayer and salvation within a philosophical context.

Carl Raschke, *Critical Theology: Introducing an Agenda for an Age of Global Crisis*, Downers Grove, IL: InterVarsity Press, 2016.

Raschke provides us with an introduction to theology from a revised critical studies perspective, drawing on the works of Slavoj Žižek and Alain Badiou in particular to engage what it means to do theology in a postsecular, postmodern age.

Joeri Schrijvers, *Between Faith and Belief: Toward a Contemporary Phenomenology of Religious Life*, Albany, NY: State University of New York Press, 2016.

By treating a host of contemporary continental philosophers of religion, such as Kearney, Caputo, Derrida, Marion, Nancy and Sloterdijk, this in-depth study of the field makes a turn toward Ludwig Binswanger's 'phenomenology of love' in order to demonstrate the possible futures of a 'contemporary phenomenology of religious life', something that elevates Schrijvers' work closer towards becoming a major force within continental thought on its own.

Joeri Schrijvers, *Ontotheological Turnings? The Decentering of the Modern Subject in Recent French Phenomenology*, Albany, NY: State University of New York Press, 2011.

Schrijvers argues in this earlier work that metaphysics and ontotheology are not entirely absent from the work of French phenomenologists such as Lacoste, Levinas, and Marion. Indeed, Schrijvers thinks that philosophy can never be fully free from metaphysics and he makes a convincing argument that such is permanently the case. This volume serves as a good introduction to the three main authors treated as well.

J. Aaron Simmons, *God and the Other: Ethics and Politics after the Theological Turn*, Bloomington, IN: Indiana University Press, 2011.

This study spends a good deal of time relating phenomenological thought to such topics as epistemology, political philosophy, and environmental ethics, all in a convincing manner, dealing specifically with Kierkegaard and Levinas in particular and asking questions about the 'Catholic' nature of continental thought.

J. Aaron Simmons and Bruce Ellis Benson, *The New Phenomenology: A Philosophical Introduction*, London: Bloomsbury, 2013.

This book presents the reader with an overview of the main figures in the 'new phenomenology', Chrétien, Derrida, Henry, Levinas, and Marion specifically. The work as a whole offers itself as an introduction that is organized thematically rather than by author so as to draw out the conversations taking place in the field more prominently. The authors also argue that the new phenomenology can productively be put into conversation with other philosophical disciplines, even those not coming out of the continental tradition.

Anthony Paul Smith and Daniel Whistler, eds., *After the Postsecular and Postmodern: Essays in Continental Philosophy of Religion*, Cambridge: Cambridge Scholars Publishing, 2011.

In their introductory chapter, Smith and Whistler argue that the encounter between theology and philosophy has not challenged theology with the same force as that which it has challenged philosophy. Calling for a richer understanding of the contribution of continental philosophy of religion, the editors have arranged the book according to themes present in the work of Gilles Deleuze. Contributors include Adam Kotsko and Clayton Crockett, among others.

Hent de Vries, *Philosophy and the Turn to Religion*, Baltimore, MD: John Hopkins University Press, 1999.

Dealing mainly with Derrida's later work on religion, though also addressing such thinkers as Levinas, Marion, and Heidegger, this book explores Derrida's writings with a particular emphasis being given to the movements of philosophy both toward and away from God. This double movement, he argues, is characteristic of the relationship between philosophy and theology, and careful study uncovers the resonance between negative theology on the one hand and deconstruction on the other.

Graham Ward, *Theology and Contemporary Critical Theory*, London: Macmillan, 1996.

> Though now over 20 years old, this introductory work manages to provide brief but substantial glimpses into the work of a variety of continental thinkers vis-à-vis theology, and thereby provides an excellent overview of much of the field. Ward manages to touch upon so many authors familiar to the present volume, including Derrida, Ricoeur, Foucault, Kristeva, Levinas, Nancy, Lyotard, Žižek and de Certeau, while also paying attention to figures not as commonly talked about, such as Irigaray, Spivak, Butler, Cixous, Stanley Fish and Hayden White.

Christopher Watkin, *Difficult Atheism: Post-Theological Thinking in Alain Badiou, Jean-Luc Nancy and Quentin Meillassoux*, Edinburgh: Edinburgh University Press, 2011.

> Christopher Watkin's main thesis is that contemporary French philosophy may not be quite as atheistic as it supposes, and so that total atheism is in fact more difficult to uphold than one might think. To each of his three title interlocutors he poses the question of whether their atheistic thought is, as some have asked, parasitic upon theological categories.

Slavoj Žižek and John Milbank, *The Monstrosity of Christ: Paradox or Dialectic?*, ed. Creston Davis, Cambridge, MA: MIT Press, 2009.

> Slavoj Žižek and John Milbank trace their fundamentally divergent visions of what Christianity is, the relationship of faith to reason, atheistic materialism as opposed to radical orthodoxy's metaphysics, and the use of dialectic as opposed to analogy in their wide-ranging and often very stimulating dialogue. Prompted by Creston Davis, who provides a good background to the conversation, these two authors see in the Incarnation a provocative, even "monstrous" event, though in radically different ways.

Slavoj Žižek, Eric Santner and Kenneth Reinhard, *The Neighbor: Three Inquires in Political Theology,* Chicago: University of Chicago Press, 2005.

> Each of these three authors provides an interesting mixture of themes and sources in order to demonstrate that contemporary continental thought has something interesting to say to the field of political theology specifically. By demonstrating this relevant connection, a vast conversation is opened up that theologians would be wise to follow up on.

Book Series
'Philosophy and Theology' series, T&T Clark/Bloomsbury.

Each volume in this series relates theology to the work of a particular philosopher. In many ways, this series is the best way to engage a particular continental philosopher in terms of the theological themes their work addresses, either directly or indirectly. Includes titles on Adorno (Christopher Craig Brittain), Agamben (Colby Dickinson), Badiou (Frederiek Depoortere), Derrida (Steven Shakespeare), Hegel (Martin J. DeNys), Heidegger (Judith Wolfe), Kierkegaard (Murray Rae), Levinas (Nigel Zimmermann), Marion (Christina M. Gschwandtner), Nietzsche (Craig Hovey), Ricoeur (Dan R. Stiver), and Žižek (Adam Kotsko), among many others.

John D. Caputo, ed., 'Perspectives in Continental Philosophy', Fordham University Press.

This series, edited by John Caputo, offers an extensive series of monographs, translated works, and edited volumes that deal exclusively with continental philosophical themes, often in relation to theological ones as well. Many of today's major continental thinkers, working from a variety of paradigms, publish their work in this series. Steadily publishing the writings of Jean-Luc Marion, Jean-Luc Nancy, Jean-Louis Chrétien, Jean-Yves Lacoste, Dominque Janicaud, Michel Henry, Claude Romano, Catherine Malabou, Emmanuel Falque, Jean Wahl and so many others. Some of its more recent publications include, *The Wedding Feast of the Lamb* (Emmanuel Falque), *Walter Benjamin and Theology* (ed. Colby Dickinson and Stéphane Symons), *Carnal Hermeneutics* (ed. Richard Kearney and Brian Treanor), *The Essential Writings* (Jean-Luc Marion, ed. Kevin Hart), *Phenomenologies of the Stranger* (ed. Richard Kearney and Kascha Semonovitch), as well as several volumes already included in this bibliography.

Jeffrey Bloechl and Kevin Hart, eds., 'Thresholds in Philosophy and Theology', University of Notre Dame Press.

This series explores the complex borders and conversations between philosophy and theology, and is an ongoing series that promises to present an interesting take on the relationship of continental thought to contemporary theological trends. Books include *Human Existence and Transcendence* (Jean Wahl), *The Contemplative Self After Michel Henry: A Phenomenological Theology* (Joseph

Rivera) and *Christianity and Secular Reason: Classical Themes and Modern Developments* (ed. Jeffrey Bloechl).

Merold Westphal, ed., Indiana Series in Philosophy of Religion.

This is a multidisciplinary series on the philosophy of religion from a continental perspective. A good deal of John Caputo's work has been published in this series, as has Richard Kearney's and, the series' editor, Merold Westphal's. As the only real rival at the moment to the Fordham University Press' 'Perspectives in Continental Philosophy', this series from Indiana University Press is an excellent resource for those interested or immersed in the fields of continental thought and theology. In addition to works already listed in the bibliography, this series includes *The Future of Continental Philosophy of Religion* (ed. Clayton Crockett, B. Keith Putt and Jeffrey Robbins), *The Insistence of God: A Theology of Perhaps* (John D. Caputo), *Transforming Philosophy and Religion: Love's Wisdom* (ed. Norman Wirzba and Bruce Ellis Benson), *Phenomenology and Mysticism: The Verticality of Religious Experience* (Anthony J. Steinbock), *Levinas and Kierkegaard in Dialogue* (Merold Westphal), and *Feminism, Sexuality, and the Return of Religion* (ed. Linda Martin Alcoff and John D. Caputo).

Slavoj Žižek, Clayton Crockett, Creston Davis, Jeffrey W. Robbins, eds., Insurrections: Critical Studies in Religion, Politics, and Culture, Columbia University Press.

A series quickly rising to prominence, 'Insurrections' has managed to cull some of the finest thinkers in the field in order to examine the intersection of religion, politics, and culture through a critical theory lens. Major contributions include authors such as Alain Badiou, François Laruelle, William Desmond, Richard Kearney, Antonio Negri, Gianni Vattimo, Catherine Keller, Stanislas Breton, Ward Blanton, Peter Sloterdijk, Catherine Malabou, as well as volumes from the series' editors, Slavoj Žižek, Jeffrey Robbins and Clayton Crockett. There is much to praise about the works in this series. Books include *Cloud of the Impossible: Negative Theology and Planetary Entanglement* (Catherine Keller) and *To Carl Schmitt: Letters and Reflections* (Jacob Taubes, trans. Keith Tribe), as well as several works already listed.

Steven Shakespeare and Duane Williams, eds., Reframing Continental Philosophy of Religion, Rowman & Littlefield.

Though a relatively new series, its stated aim is to bring new voices and methods to the study of continental philosophy of religion. In addition to *Speculation,*

Heresy and Gnosis in Contemporary Philosophy of Religion: The Enigmatic Absolute (ed. Joshua Ramey and Matthew S. Haar Farris), the series currently includes *Simone Weil and Continental Philosophy* (ed. Rebecca A. Rozelle-Stone).

SUNY series in Theology and Continental Thought

Demonstrating that there is much good to be expected from a smaller compilation of studies, this series includes some wonderful works in the field by Joeri Schrijvers and Thomas J.J. Altizer, among others. Titles include *Between Faith and Belief: Toward a Contemporary Phenomenology of Religious Life* (Joeri Schrijvers), *Satan and Apocalypse* (Thomas J.J. Altizer), *A Passion for the Impossible: John D. Caputo in Focus* (ed. Mark Dooley) and *Thinking Through the Death of God: A Critical Companion to Thomas J.J. Altizer* (ed. Lissa McCullough and Brian Schroeder).